WEAPONS OF TERROR

Freeing the World of Nuclear, Biological and Chemical Arms

D1402245

WEAPONS OF TERROR

Freeing the World of Nuclear, Biological and Chemical Arms

THE WEAPONS OF
MASS DESTRUCTION
COMMISSION

www.wmdcommission.org

This publication may be reproduced in full or in
part if accompanied with the following citation:
Weapons of Mass Destruction Commission,
final report, 'Weapons of Terror: Freeing the World
of Nuclear, Biological, and Chemical Arms',
Stockholm, Sweden, 1 june 2006.

For electronic copies of this report, please visit
www.wmdcommission.org.

ISBN: 91-38-22582-4

Printing: EO Grafiska, Stockholm
Design: Fidelity Stockholm AB
Photo: NASA/Roger Ressmeyer/Corbis

Contents

Abbreviations

ABM	Anti-ballistic missile
ASAT	Anti-satellite (weapon)
BMD	Ballistic missile defence
BW	Biological weapon/warfare
BTWC	Biological and Toxin Weapons Convention
CBM	Confidence-building measure
CBW	Chemical and biological weapons
CD	Conference on Disarmament
CFE	Conventional Armed Forces in Europe (Treaty)
CTBT	Comprehensive Nuclear-Test-Ban Treaty
CTBTO	Comprehensive Nuclear-Test-Ban Treaty Organization
CTR	Cooperative threat reduction
CW	Chemical weapon/warfare
CWC	Chemical Weapons Convention
FAO	Food and Agriculture Organization
FMCT	Fissile material cut-off treaty
G8	Group of Eight, group of eight leading industrialized states
GTRI	Global Threat Reduction Initiative
HCOC	Hague Code of Conduct
HEU	Highly enriched uranium
IAEA	International Atomic Energy Agency
ICBM	Intercontinental ballistic missile
ICJ	International Court of Justice
INF	Intermediate-range Nuclear Forces (Treaty)
LEU	Low-enriched uranium
MAD	Mutual assured destruction
MIRV	Multiple, independently targetable re-entry vehicle
MTCR	Missile Technology Control Regime
NASA	National Aeronautics and Space Administration (US)
NATO	North Atlantic Treaty Organization
NBC	Nuclear/biological/chemical
NGO	Non-governmental organization
NPT	Non-Proliferation Treaty
NSG	Nuclear Suppliers Group
NWFZ	Nuclear-weapon-free zone
NWS	Nuclear-weapon state

OIE	World Organisation for Animal Health
OPCW	Organisation for the Prohibition of Chemical Weapons
P5	Five permanent members of the United Nations Security Council
PSI	Proliferation Security Initiative
PTBT	Partial Test-Ban Treaty (Treaty Banning Nuclear Weapon Tests in the Atmosphere, in Outer Space and Under Water)
SARS	Severe acute respiratory syndrome
SALT I, II, (III)	Strategic Arms Limitation Treaty (Soviet-US)
SIPRI	Stockholm International Peace Research Institute
SLBM	Submarine-launched ballistic missile
SORT	Strategic Offensive Reductions Treaty
SSOD	Special Session on Disarmament (of the UN General Assembly)
START	Strategic Arms Reduction Treaty
UAV	Unmanned aerial vehicle
UNDC	United Nations Disarmament Commission
UNDDA	United Nations Department for Disarmament Affairs
UNGA	United Nations General Assembly
UNIDIR	United Nations Institute for Disarmament Research
UNMOVIC	United Nations Monitoring, Verification and Inspection Commission
UNSC	United Nations Security Council
UNSCOM	United Nations Special Commission on Iraq
WHO	World Health Organization
WMD	Weapon(s) of mass destruction
WMDC	Weapons of Mass Destruction Commission

Chairman's preface

IN SEPTEMBER 2003, the Swedish Foreign Minister, Anna Lindh, was brutally killed. Inspirational, young and full of initiative, she would have had much more to contribute to making the world a better place.

During the first months of 2003, Anna phoned me from time to time to inform herself about the United Nations inspection work in Iraq, for which I was responsible. She and many of her colleagues were very unhappy about the drift towards military action against Iraq and felt that the inspectors should be given more time for their search for weapons of mass destruction. She also felt, however, that a sceptical attitude to armed action was not enough. It had to be matched by more active policies on the issue of non-proliferation. I fully agreed with her and was pleased to see that in June 2003 she and her colleagues in the European Union declared new joint policies.

These policies, in my view, started from sensible premises: that the best solution to the problem of the proliferation of weapons of mass destruction was that countries should no longer feel that they needed them; and that violators should be encouraged to walk back and rejoin the international community. These policies stressed the need for a cooperative approach to collective security and a rule-based international order. They highlighted the role of international verification and 'effective multilateralism'. They also supported, as a last resort, however, the position that coercive measures under Chapter VII of the United Nations Charter could be taken with the Security Council as the final arbiter.

By the end of June 2003, when the occupation of Iraq was a fact and I was leaving the UN, Anna Lindh contacted me again. She thought that the time was right not only for the new European policies but also for an idea first advanced by Jayantha Dhanapala, then UN Under-Secretary-General for Disarmament: the creation of an independent international commission to examine how the world could tackle the problem of weapons of mass destruction. She asked if I would chair such a commission. I said I would.

After Anna Lindh's death, the Swedish Prime Minister, Göran Persson, and Anna's successor as Foreign Minister, Laila Freivalds, gave me a free hand to establish the Commission. I have been fortunate to secure the participation of high-calibre members, who have contributed their ideas, knowledge, judgement – and texts. They have all taken part in practical political, diplomatic or military work related to the maintenance of peace and the reduction of armaments. The Commission has not aimed at utopian goals but has ardently and jointly sought to exercise judgement and point to constructive avenues out of difficulties, which are still with us. While this preface is mine, the report and its recommendations reflect the joint effort of the Commission.

The Swedish Government has generously financed most of the costs of the Commission and – as separately acknowledged – several other governments and other sources have kindly contributed, especially the Simons Foundation in Vancouver, Canada.

Three previous independent international commissions have presented valuable reports in the same field.

In 1982, a commission headed by Prime Minister Olof Palme of Sweden submitted a report entitled *Common Security*. It argued that the nuclear arms race and mutual assured destruction (MAD) could destroy human civilization and that security could only be attained through cooperation and disarmament. It pinned its hopes on the strong antiwar opinion, which feared nuclear annihilation. Although the Cold War continued, significant bilateral arms control agreements were concluded between the United States and the Soviet Union, and the Helsinki Conference on Security and Co-operation in Europe was a harbinger of a new climate.

In 1996, there appeared the Australian Government-sponsored *Report of the Canberra Commission on the Elimination of Nuclear Weapons*. After the end of the Cold War, this was a period of bright hope. After the successful UN-authorized Gulf War in 1991, which stopped Iraq's aggression against Kuwait, President George H.W. Bush talked about 'a new world order'. The indefinite extension of the Non-Proliferation Treaty was achieved in 1995 after commitments to nuclear disarmament had been reaffirmed by the five nuclear-weapon states parties to the treaty. The Canberra Commission urged that practical steps to eliminate nuclear weapons should be taken immediately.

In August 1998, just months after Pakistan's and India's nuclear tests, the Government of Japan organized the independent Tokyo Forum for Nuclear Non-Proliferation and Diasarmament. Its final report, issued a year later, presented an 'Action Plan' dealing with nuclear disarmament, non-proliferation and terrorism.

Soon thereafter, however, the US Senate declined to support ratification of the Comprehensive Nuclear-Test-Ban Treaty. With little or no progress on nuclear disarmament, nuclear proliferation an ongoing reality, and growing fears of the dangers of terrorism, the post-Cold War window of opportunity was closing, even despite other more positive trends.

In the ten years that have passed since the Canberra Commission report was published, global economic interdependence has accelerated. All states of the world have come to face the same environmental threats and risks of contagious diseases. There have been no serious territorial or ideological conflicts between the major military powers. Yet, amazingly, the climate for agreements on arms control and disarmament has actually deteriorated.

Efforts to consolidate global treaties, like the Nuclear Non-Proliferation Treaty and the Biological and Toxin Weapons Convention, have stagnated, ratifications of the Comprehensive Nuclear-Test-Ban Treaty remain missing, and negotiations have not even opened on the much needed treaty to stop the production of fissile material for weapons.

There are even some waves of new armaments: the US missile shield may be triggering countermeasures by China and Russia in the nuclear weapons area; and nuclear weapons with new missions may be developed in the US and elsewhere. While the peaceful uses of space and satellites are developing at a dizzying pace, facilitating global information and communication, the most advanced military powers are calculating how they can most effectively pursue war in this environment.

In spite of all this, governments and world public opinion are paying less attention to the global regimes for arms control and disarmament. One reason is the intense and justified focus on the war on terrorism and the handling of specific cases of actual or potential nuclear proliferation. Another reason may be that global treaties did not help to prevent the terrorist attack on the United States on 11 September 2001 and constituted insufficient barriers against the efforts of Iraq, North Korea and Libya to acquire nuclear weapons and against Iran to conceal a programme for the enrichment of uranium.

While the reaction of most states to the treaty violations was to strengthen and develop the existing treaties and institutions, the US, the sole superpower, has looked more to its own military power for remedies. The US National Security Strategy of 2002 made it clear that the US would feel free to use armed force without authorization of the United Nations Security Council to counter not only an actual or imminent attack involving WMD but also a WMD threat that might be uncertain as to time and place. The declared US policy – reaffirmed on this point by the strategy issued in March 2006 – has, as I see it, parted ways with the UN Charter provisions on self-defence. The aim of the strategy was said to be '*to help make the world not just safer but better*', indicating that the US believed that this policy had benefits for all.

No one underestimates the difficulties on the road to disarmament and to outlawing nuclear weapons in the same manner in which the other weapons of terror – biological and chemical weapons – have been outlawed.

Some of the current stagnation in global arms control and disarmament forums is the result of a paralysing requirement of consensus combined with an outdated system of bloc politics. However, a more important reason is that the nuclear-weapon states no longer seem to take their commitment to nuclear disarmament seriously – even though this was an essential part of the NPT bargain, both at the treaty's birth in 1968 and when it was extended indefinitely in 1995.

The devaluation of international commitments inherent in these positions risks undermining the credibility and effectiveness of multilateral treaty commitments.

Against a generally gloomy short-term outlook for arms control and disarmament, some positive features can be discerned in the broader field of security. The number of interstate armed conflicts has been declining. Peace-keeping operations have prevented and continue to prevent shooting wars in many places. Efforts to reform the UN have borne some fruit and more may be hoped for. The new UN Peacebuilding Commission will assist states emerging from conflicts, thereby reducing the risk of their relapse into violence.

The Security Council has recently adopted an important resolution obligating member states to adopt domestic legislation designed to prevent the proliferation of WMD. The precedent is constructive. But if the Council were to further use and develop its quasi-legislative potential, it would need to ensure that it acts with the broad support of the UN members. In the longer run this would entail making the Council more representative of the UN membership.

Lastly, in today's rapidly integrating world community, global treaties and global institutions, like the UN, the IAEA and the OPCW, remain indispensable. Even with their shortcomings they can do some important things that states acting alone cannot achieve. They are therefore essential instruments in the hands of the state community to enhance security, to jointly operate inspection systems and to reduce the threat of weapons of mass destruction. Governments that have shown disenchantment with global treaties and institutions will inevitably return and renew their engagement.

When there is a greater general readiness to return to a cooperative multi-lateral system in the sphere of arms control and disarmament, the Commission's report, I hope, will contribute to the practical agenda. Some ideas and recommendations are new, but the Commission also espouses and argues in favour of some well-known existing proposals.

Indeed, at the present time it seems to me that not only successes in the vital work to prevent proliferation and terrorism but also progress in two additional areas could transform the current gloom into hope. Bringing the Comprehensive Nuclear-Test-Ban Treaty into force would significantly impede the development of new nuclear weapons. The weapons that exist today are bad enough. Negotiating a global treaty to stop the production of fissile material for weapons would close the tap for new such material and help hinder possible arms races – notably in Asia.

In both these areas the US has the decisive leverage. If it takes the lead the world is likely to follow. If it does not take the lead, there could be more nuclear tests and new nuclear arms races.

Hans Blix
WMDC Chairman
May 2006

WEAPONS OF TERROR
Freeing the World of Nuclear, Biological and Chemical Arms

Synopsis

WHY ACTION IS NECESSARY

- Nuclear, biological and chemical arms are the most inhumane of all weapons. Designed to terrify as well as destroy, they can, in the hands of either states or non-state actors, cause destruction on a vastly greater scale than any conventional weapons, and their impact is far more indiscriminate and long-lasting.
- So long as any state has such weapons – especially nuclear arms – others will want them. So long as any such weapons remain in any state's arsenal, there is a high risk that they will one day be used, by design or accident. Any such use would be catastrophic.
- Notwithstanding the end of the Cold War balance of terror, stocks of such weapons remain extraordinarily and alarmingly high: some 27,000 in the case of nuclear weapons, of which around 12,000 are still actively deployed.
- Weapons of mass destruction cannot be uninvented. But they can be outlawed, as biological and chemical weapons already have been, and their use made unthinkable. Compliance, verification and enforcement rules can, with the requisite will, be effectively applied. And with that will, even the eventual elimination of nuclear weapons is not beyond the world's reach.
- Over the past decade, there has been a serious, and dangerous, loss of momentum and direction in disarmament and non-proliferation efforts. Treaty making and implementation have stalled and, as a new wave of proliferation has threatened, unilateral enforcement action has been increasingly advocated.
- In 2005 there were two loud wake-up calls in the failure of the NPT Review Conference and in the inability of the World Summit to agree on a single line about any WMD issue. It is critical for those calls to be heeded now.

WHAT MUST BE DONE

The Weapons of Mass Destruction Commission makes many specific and detailed recommendations throughout its report (see Annex 1 for a consolidated list). The most important of them are summarized below.

1   Agree on general principles of action

- Disarmament and non-proliferation are best pursued through a cooperative rule-based international order, applied and enforced through effective multilateral institutions, with the UN Security Council as the ultimate global authority.
- There is an urgent need to revive meaningful negotiations, through all available intergovernmental mechanisms, on the three main objectives of reducing the danger of present arsenals, preventing proliferation, and outlawing all weapons of mass destruction once and for all.
- States, individually and collectively, should consistently pursue policies designed to ensure that no state feels a need to acquire weapons of mass destruction.
- Governments and relevant intergovernmental organizations and non-government actors should commence preparations for a World Summit on disarmament, non-proliferation and terrorist use of weapons of mass destruction to generate new momentum for concerted international action.

2   Reduce the danger of present arsenals: no use by states – no access by terrorists

- Secure all weapons of mass destruction and all WMD-related material and equipment from theft or other acquisition by terrorists.
- Take nuclear weapons off high-alert status to reduce the risk of launching by error; make deep reductions in strategic nuclear weapons; place all non-strategic nuclear weapons in centralized storage; and withdraw all such weapons from foreign soil.
- Prohibit the production of fissile material for nuclear weapons, and phase out the production of highly enriched uranium.
- Diminish the role of nuclear weapons by making no-first-use pledges, by giving assurances not to use them against non-nuclear-weapon states, and by not developing nuclear weapons for new tasks.

3   Prevent proliferation: no new weapon systems – no new possessors

- Prohibit any nuclear-weapon tests by bringing the Comprehensive Nuclear-Test-Ban Treaty into force.
- Revive the fundamental commitments of all NPT parties: the five nuclear-weapon states to negotiate towards nuclear disarmament and the non-nuclear-weapon states to refrain from developing nuclear weapons.
- Recognize that countries that are not party to the NPT also have a duty to participate in the disarmament process.
- Continue negotiations with Iran and North Korea to achieve their effective and verified rejection of the nuclear-weapon option, while assuring their security and acknowledging the right of all NPT parties to peaceful uses of nuclear energy.
- Explore international arrangements for an assurance of supply of enriched uranium fuel, and for the disposal of spent fuel, to reduce incentives for national facilities and to diminish proliferation risks.

4   Work towards outlawing all weapons of mass destruction once and for all

- Accept the principle that nuclear weapons should be outlawed, as are biological and chemical weapons, and explore the political, legal, technical and procedural options for achieving this within a reasonable time.
- Complete the implementation of existing regional nuclear-weapon-free zones and work actively to establish zones free of WMD in other regions, particularly and most urgently in the Middle East.
- Achieve universal compliance with, and effective implementation of, the Chemical Weapons Convention, and speed up the destruction of chemical weapon stocks.
- Achieve universal compliance with, and effective implementation of, the Biological and Toxin Weapons Convention, and improve cooperation between industry, scientists and governments to reinforce the ban on the development and production of biological weapons and to keep abreast of developments in biotechnology.
- Prevent an arms race in space by prohibiting any stationing or use of weapons in outer space.

Reviving disarmament

Reviving disarmament

Nuclear, biological and chemical weapons are rightly called weapons of mass destruction (WMD). Designed to terrify as well as destroy, they have the potential to kill thousands and thousands of people in a single attack, and their effects may persist in the environment and in our bodies, in some cases indefinitely.

Many efforts have been made to free the world from the threat of these weapons and some progress has been made. Paradoxically, despite the end of the Cold War, the past decade has seen more setbacks than successes. States have failed to comply with their disarmament and non-proliferation commitments, and terrorist groups have emerged that recognize no restraints.

In September 2005, the United Nations World Summit was unable to agree on a single recommendation on disarmament and non-proliferation.

It is time for all to wake up to the awesome reality that many of the old threats continue to hang over the world and that many new ones have emerged.

It is time for all governments to revive their cooperation and to breathe new life into the disarmament work of the United Nations. Efforts to eradicate poverty and to protect the global environment must be matched by a dismantling of the world's most destructive capabilities. The gearshift now needs to be moved from reverse to drive.

Biological and chemical weapons have been comprehensively outlawed through global conventions, but these need to be universally accepted and fully implemented. Nuclear weapons must also be outlawed. Before this aim is realized, there must be new initiatives to reduce the number of nuclear weapons and the threat posed by them. It is equally urgent to prevent proliferation and to take special measures to ensure that terrorists do not acquire any weapons of mass destruction.

This report presents ideas and recommendations on what the world community – including national governments and civil society – can and should do.

WHY WEAPONS OF MASS DESTRUCTION MATTER

Why not discuss small arms, which currently are causing the greatest number of victims? Or napalm, phosphorus or cluster bombs, which may cause excessive suffering or have indiscriminate effects?

It is not a question of either/or. The Commission focuses on weapons of mass destruction, which is a big enough challenge. Other institutions address the problems of other weapons and methods of warfare.

There are significant differences in the use, effects, legal status and strategic importance of nuclear, biological and chemical weapons. Nuclear weapons continue to pose the most dramatic threats. Some experts regard the differences as so significant that they will not lump the three types of weapons together under the single term of WMD. Nevertheless, as weapons of terror all three categories fall under the same stigma, which makes it logical to deal with them as a group.

There are a number of major reasons why the present general standstill in global talks is unacceptable and why governments must refocus on WMD and revive efforts to achieve disarmament, arms control, non-proliferation and compliance:

- The development of chemical science and industry as well as the rapid expansion in biotechnology and life sciences create opportunities for important peaceful uses, but also for the production of chemical weapons and horrific uses of viruses and bacteria as weapons.
- The terror attacks on the United States on 11 September 2001 demonstrated to the world in a flash that, if terrorists succeed in acquiring WMD, they might use them.
- The 1968 Non-Proliferation Treaty (NPT), while recognizing the first wave of five nuclear-weapon states, succeeded in attracting a vast number of adherents. It did not, however, prevent India, Israel and Pakistan from forming a second wave of proliferation, and was violated by Iraq, Libya and North Korea in a third wave. If Iran and North Korea do not reliably renounce nuclear weapons, pressure could build for a fourth wave of proliferation of nuclear weapons.
- Thirty-six years after the entry into force of the NPT, the five nuclear-weapon states parties to the treaty have failed in their duty to achieve disarmament through negotiation. There is currently a risk for a new phase in nuclear arms competition through the further modernization of weapons. Many non-nuclear-weapon states feel cheated by the nuclear-weapon states' retreating from commitments made in 1995 in order to get the treaty extended to unlimited duration.

- The IAEA safeguards system, created to verify that no nuclear material is diverted from peaceful uses, proved inadequate to discover the Iraqi and Libyan violations of the NPT. Iran failed for many years in its duty to declare important nuclear programmes.
- The know-how to make nuclear, biological and chemical weapons and weapons-usable material – enriched uranium or plutonium, modified viruses and precursor chemicals – is available to a widening group of states and non-state actors.
- Rapid changes in the life sciences influence the availability of the information and expertise required to make toxins and genetically modified viruses and other pathogens.
- The existence of an illicit private global market where WMD expertise, technology, material and designs for weapons could be acquired is a special threat at a time of active worldwide terrorism.
- The expansion expected in the use of carbon-dioxide-free nuclear power will lead to the production, transportation and use of more nuclear fuel, increasing the risk that enriched uranium and plutonium might be diverted to weapons. Radioactive substances or nuclear waste not under full control might be acquired by terrorists and be used in dirty bombs – devices that disperse radioactive material to contaminate target areas or to provoke terror.

DISARMAMENT IN DISARRAY

Many people thought that the end of the Cold War would make global agreements on disarmament easier to conclude and implement. Many also expected that public opinion would push for this. The opposite has been the case. After the promising conclusion of the Chemical Weapons Convention and the indefinite extension of the NPT in the early and mid-1990s, other vital global agreements on disarmament and arms control remain unratified, like the Comprehensive Nuclear-Test-Ban Treaty (CTBT), or not negotiated, like the fissile material cut-off treaty (FMCT). Efforts at arms control and disarmament between the United States and Russia have similarly come to a standstill; some measures have been reversed. The US unilaterally terminated the Anti-Ballistic Missile (ABM) Treaty in order to proceed with the construction of a missile shield. The START II Treaty became a casualty, as did the framework for a START III treaty that was agreed in Helsinki in 1997 by Presidents Clinton and Yeltsin.

Some of the current setbacks in treaty-based arms control and disarmament can be traced to a pattern in US policy that is sometimes called 'selective multilateralism' – an increased US scepticism regarding the effectiveness of international institutions and instruments, coupled with a drive for freedom of action to maintain an absolute global superiority in weaponry and means of their delivery.

The US is clearly less interested in global approaches and treaty making than it was in the Cold War era. In the case of Iraq, the US chose in 2003 to rely on its own national intelligence and to disregard the results of international verification, even though the latter turned out to be more accurate. More importantly, the US has been looking to what is called 'counter-proliferation' – a policy envisaging the unilateral use of force – as a chief means to deal with perceived nuclear or other WMD threats. As seen in the war to eliminate WMD in Iraq, and in official statements regarding North Korea and Iran, the US has claimed a right to take armed action if necessary to remove what it perceives as growing threats, even without the authorization of the UN Security Council.

The overwhelming majority of states reject the claims by the US or any other state to such a wide licence on the use of force. While they recognize the right for states under Article 51 of the UN Charter to take armed action in self-defence against an *imminent* threat, they share the view expressed in 2004 by the UN Secretary-General's High-level Panel on Threats, Challenges and Change that, in cases where the threat is not imminent, there is an obligation – and time – to turn to the Security Council to ask for authorization for the use of armed force. On this matter, the Commission notes the fundamental difference between what may be termed the 'unilateralist' approach of the current US Administration and the 'multilateralist' approach of most of the rest of the world.

The vast majority of states still give their primary support to cooperative approaches based on treaty making combined with practical action within international organizations. They see themselves as stakeholders in jointly managed systems of treaties and organizations for disarmament, arms control, verification and the building of security. Rather than downgrading these efforts, they wish to remedy their weaknesses and further develop and strengthen them. They do not accept a de facto perpetuation of a licence for five – or more – states to possess nuclear weapons, and they resist measures that would expand the inequality that exists between the nuclear haves and have-nots. Renouncing nuclear weapons for themselves, they wish to see steps that will lead to the outlawing of nuclear weapons for all.

THE AIM AND APPROACH OF THIS REPORT

Cooperative action: This report argues for the aim of outlawing all weapons of mass destruction. It concentrates on what could and should be short- and medium-term steps in this direction. The Commission takes the view that, while many unilateral, bilateral and regional steps and measures are needed and helpful, the abhorrence of the peoples of all nations of weapons of mass destruction requires an approach that builds on the cooperation and support of the entire world community. Regimes that invite and encourage the adherence of all states must be established and managed on a global scale. Treaties and international organizations, notably the United Nations, are indispensable tools and forums.

Despite current controversies, there are grounds for hope about the longer-term future of arms control and disarmament. In this first decade of the new millennium, the interdependence of states and peoples is accelerating at an unprecedented pace. Closer relationships in trade, finance, information and communications offer means through which international influence and pressure can be exercised without any resort to force. Admittedly, there is also a dark side to this: as borders become more porous and communications easier, terrorists, criminals and weapons proliferators have an easier time. These are problems that the UN Secretary-General described as 'problems without passports'.

While only 20 years elapsed between the First and the Second World War, 60 years have now passed without direct armed confrontations between the great powers. UN peacekeeping operations and peace building are playing a crucial role both in preventing hostilities and in restoring peace in places of conflict. The number of interstate wars has declined nearly every year over the past two decades. Most armed conflicts are now within states. Although often gravely violated, the fabric of international rules on human rights amounts to a codification of values held in common by all peoples – a nascent globalization of ethics. Doubtless, while people will always have their ideological and national differences, the vast majority of humanity appears to be seeking the benefits of an increasingly interdependent world and is not rallying to the idea of an inevitable clash of civilizations.

The Commission is convinced that global and regional institutions will prove indispensable in managing this growing interdependence. Just as many problems within states cannot be solved at the local level but require a national approach, many problems at the national level cannot be solved independently but require an international approach. This is true for the prevention not only of diseases, but also of threats to the environment and certainly for the threats posed by weapons of mass destruction. The measure of restraint and cooperation that such a system will require of individual states – including the biggest and strongest – is compensated by results that cannot be achieved by solo actions.

To meet three major challenges: This report focuses on three principal types of challenge posed by the existence of WMD in the current security environment: existing arsenals, possible new possessor states, and possible non-state possessors.

The challenge of existing WMD arsenals. The lower political and military tension between the great powers, since the collapse of the Soviet Union, largely remains. Although military expenditures have risen in some countries, notably the United States, they have been reduced in many other states. There are no major territorial disputes between the great powers, and no one expects war to occur between them.

Yet, they maintain or are modernizing their strategic capabilities. The US development of a shield against incoming missiles is viewed with much distrust by China and Russia as possibly affecting the deterrent capacity of their nuclear forces. The nuclear de-escalation and reductions that have taken place so far are welcome, but one must be aware that part of this is only a removal of redundancies.

The challenge that additional states may acquire WMD. Iraq and Libya were made to retreat on this path. Intense efforts are being made to bring North Korea to do the same and to dissuade Iran from moving forward. It is these cases that have led to fears that the NPT may unravel. While the world community has reason to be alarmed by these cases, it also has reason to assess the risks of proliferation soberly. The world is not milling with states tempted to acquire WMD as soon as the opportunity is there. Indeed, some states have voluntarily eliminated the nuclear weapons that they had. An even larger number of states have rejected any acquisition of nuclear, chemical and biological weapons and are abiding by their commitments.

They may do so for a variety of reasons: an absence of perceived threats, a lack of technical capability and a wish to join the global effort to rid the world of weapons that they find abhorrent. The greatest challenge in the process of disarmament is to pursue political developments, globally and regionally, that make all states feel secure without WMD.

The challenge that terrorists may get access to WMD. Past experience, suggesting that there is limited interest in these weapons by non-state actors, is no safe guide for the future. Their use of WMD could occur either within a state or across borders. In either case, terrorists must have their feet on the ground somewhere. It is important to insist, therefore, on the duty of all states to prevent their territory from being used as a base for such activities. Where borders are porous or government authority is weak, outside assistance should be offered. There is broad support for many measures, like improved control over nuclear and other dangerous materials, and strengthened international cooperation between police, intelligence and financial institutions. Also needed are domestic and foreign policies that do not lead groups of people to turn to terrorism out of a sense of despair or humiliation.

The long impasse in the cooperation to strengthen global treaties on arms control and disarmament, and to develop new instruments, has resulted in insecurity and vast resources being spent on arms races. What we now need are fresh thinking and fresh assessments of what could and should be done to revive the process. This report seeks to supply some such ideas and present recommendations. In the process of shaping them, the Commission has been guided by several essential considerations:

- **Balance, impartiality and universality.** The Commission views all WMD as inherently dangerous, in anybody's hands, especially but not only in the possession of governments acting recklessly or of terrorist groups. The Commission's aim has been to undertake a factual and impartial analysis and, on that basis, to place responsibility for pursuing solutions on all relevant actors.
- **The reduction and elimination of WMD must be pursued through measures at all stages** of the life cycle of WMD – from their creation and deployment to their disposal and destruction.
- **There must be no compromise on the goal of outlawing nuclear weapons.** This goal was accepted as a legally binding commitment as early as 1970, when the NPT entered into force. There can be no going back from it, and all steps in the disarmament process must be taken with this goal in view.
- **Many proposals that have not yet been acted upon remain highly relevant.** This report does not hesitate to endorse such proposals, when it finds them constructive. It took some 20 years to complete the Chemical Weapons Convention and four decades to reach agreement to end nuclear testing.

- **Everyone must contribute.** WMD constitute challenges not just for governments and international organizations. Research communities, non-governmental organizations, civil society, businesses, the media and the general public share ownership of the WMD challenges. They must all be allowed and encouraged to contribute to solutions. The report looks to them to discuss, to review and ultimately to promote its recommendations.

Weapons of terror: threats and responses

CHAPTER 2

Weapons of terror: threats and responses

For more than 100 years, humanity has sought to outlaw weapons and methods of war with indiscriminate or particularly cruel effects – weapons of mass destruction and terror. The first Hague Peace Conference, held in 1899, adopted several rules for this purpose. After the extensive use of gas during the First World War, states bound themselves in the 1925 Geneva Protocol to prohibit the use of both chemical and biological weapons. In the closing days of the Second World War, Hiroshima and Nagasaki were incinerated with nuclear weapons. Since then, efforts have been under way worldwide to control their numbers, prevent their spread, prohibit their use and eliminate them.

BOX 1

THE LETHAL EFFECTS OF WEAPONS OF MASS DESTRUCTION (WMD)

- **Nuclear weapons** kill by the effects of heat, blast, radiation and radio-active fallout. The attacks on Hiroshima and Nagasaki killed an estimated 200,000 people, virtually all civilians. The nuclear weapons in one strategic submarine have a combined explosive force several times greater than all the conventional bombs dropped in World War II.

- **Biological and toxin weapons** kill by using pathogens to attack cells and organs in human bodies, although they can also be used to target crops and livestock on a massive scale. Some are contagious and can spread rapidly in a population, while others, including anthrax and ricin, infect and kill only those who are directly exposed. *Toxins* are poisons produced by biological organisms. Some (e.g. botulinum toxin) are lethal even in microscopic amounts.

- **Chemical weapons** kill by attacking the nervous system and lungs, or by interfering with a body's ability to absorb oxygen. Some are designed to incapacitate by producing severe burns and blisters. Symptoms can appear immediately or be delayed for up to 12 hours after an attack. Persistent agents can remain in a target environment for as long as a week.

The Charter of the United Nations, adopted six weeks before the bombing of the two Japanese cities, does not contain any article specifically dealing with weapons of mass destruction. However, Article 11 authorizes the General Assembly to consider 'the principles governing disarmament and the regulation of armaments' and empowers it to make recommendations with regard to such principles to the Member States or the Security Council, or both. Article 26 gives the Security Council the responsibility 'for formulating ... plans to be submitted to the Members of the United Nations for the establishment of a system for the regulation of armaments'.

While the Security Council has not so far embarked on armaments regulation, it has on many occasions, as described in this report, dealt with matters relating to weapons of mass destruction. Over the years the General Assembly has been deeply engaged in 'disarmament and the regulation of armaments', including questions relating to weapons of mass destruction.

On 24 January 1946, the very first resolution adopted by the General Assembly called for 'the elimination from national armaments of atomic weapons and of all other major weapons adaptable to mass destruction'. While the world has still not achieved this goal, it has made significant progress, notably through the adoption of three major multilateral treaties (see Box 2), which are discussed in greater detail in the following chapters.

Together, these three treaties provide the basic building blocks of the global effort to address threats posed by WMD. They are not, however, the only instruments and means available. In fact, there is great variety both in the types of WMD threats facing the world and in the individual and collective responses chosen by states to address them.

THE NATURE OF THREATS FROM WEAPONS OF MASS DESTRUCTION

To counteract threats of WMD it is important to assess them accurately and to understand what motivates states or non-state actors to acquire them. Without the right diagnosis, it is unlikely that the right therapy will be found. The erroneous assessment that Iraq possessed WMD was the principal justification given for sending hundreds of thousands of soldiers to invade Iraq in 2003 – only to find no WMD.

Assessing the threats may be difficult. The secrecy often maintained about WMD programmes is one evident reason. Another reason is that threats are sometimes exaggerated – or ignored – as a part of the military-political play

BOX 2

THREE KEY GLOBAL WMD TREATIES

Treaty on the Non-Proliferation of Nuclear Weapons (NPT)

The NPT seeks to prevent the further spread of nuclear weapons, to promote cooperation in the peaceful uses of nuclear energy, and to pursue nuclear disarmament. It entered into force in 1970. In 1995, the duration of the NPT was extended indefinitely. 189 parties have joined the NPT, including the five nuclear-weapon states China, France, Russia, the UK and the US. India, Israel and Pakistan have not joined. and North Korea has announced its withdrawal from the treaty. More countries have acceded to the NPT than to any other arms limitation or disarmament agreement. The NPT represents the only binding commitment in a multilateral treaty to the goal of disarmament by the nuclear-weapon states.

Convention on the Prohibition of the Development, Production and Stockpiling of Bacteriological (Biological) and Toxin Weapons and on their Destruction (BTWC)

The BTWC is the first multilateral disarmament treaty banning the acquisition and retention of an entire category of weapons of mass destruction. It builds on the ban on the use of such weapons contained in the 1925 Geneva Protocol. The BTWC entered into force in 1975. No agreement has been reached on a verification regime to monitor compliance with the Convention. The BTWC has 155 states parties.

Convention on the Prohibition of the Development, Production, Stockpiling and Use of Chemical Weapons and on Their Destruction (CWC)

The CWC bans the development, production, stockpiling, transfer and use of chemical weapons. It entered into force in 1997. The CWC has 178 states parties. CWC parties are required to declare any chemical weapons-related activities, to secure and destroy any stockpiles of chemical weapons within stipulated deadlines, as well as to inactivate and eliminate any chemical-weapons production capacity within their jurisdiction. Six states parties have declared chemical weapons. The CWC is the first disarmament agreement to require the elimination of an entire category of weapons of mass destruction under universally applied international control. Its operative functions are carried out by the OPCW (Organisation for the Prohibition of Chemical Weapons).

between states or in the politicking within states. A third reason is that a threat consists not only of a capability but also of an intent – that may change over time. A special difficulty arises in assessing low-probability but high-consequence threats, such as the danger of terrorists acquiring nuclear weapons.

It is often assumed that perceived security interests are the prime motivation for states to seek or to retain WMD. It is true that WMD programmes in one state, if perceived as a threat to some other state or states, have a tendency to prompt other WMD programmes – as seen in the countries that followed the United States into the nuclear club after 1945, in the reciprocal nuclear tests in South Asia in 1998, and in persisting WMD-related developments in the Middle East.

Some states might view WMD, especially nuclear weapons, as a way of balancing an overwhelming conventional superiority of an adversary. NATO long used this balance-of-terror rationale to counter the Soviet Union's perceived superiority in conventional forces. The same logic is now followed by Russia, which maintains that its tactical nuclear weapons are needed to balance a perceived superiority of NATO's conventional forces. States might also view WMD as a hedge against some perceived future or emerging security threat.

Yet security is not the only motivation for states to seek WMD. A state could also seek such weapons in the belief that this would enhance its prestige or standing. It could also pursue WMD in response to domestic political pressures or advocacy from within government bureaucracies or specialized weapons labs.

While the list of possible motivations is long, fortunately the list of countries that have acquired such weapons has remained shorter than was once feared. Undoubtedly, one reason is that, while the technical capability to develop and deliver WMD is spreading, nuclear weapons in particular are still beyond the reach of many states. Another explanation is that most states have concluded that WMD are both abhorrent and unnecessary to meet their own security interests.

Nevertheless, the very existence of WMD, regardless of whose hands they are in, poses some risks and remains a potential deadly threat. Intentions, as governments, change over time.

For each of the three types of WMD the Commission addresses three main categories of threat:

- from existing weapons;
- from their spread to additional states (proliferation);
- from their possible acquisition or use by terrorists.

Nuclear-weapon threats

Existing weapons

Despite Post-Cold War reductions, some 12,000 nuclear weapons remain in active service ('deployed'). Over 90 percent of those weapons are in the arsenals of the United States and Russia (see Figure 1).

The total of both deployed and non-deployed weapons is estimated to be in the vicinity of 27,000.[1] The lack of precision in the number of these weapons (and fissile material stocks) reflects the fragmentary nature of the published information about existing nuclear arsenals. This limited transparency has many implications, including the difficulties it creates for measuring progress in achieving disarmament goals and ensuring accountability.

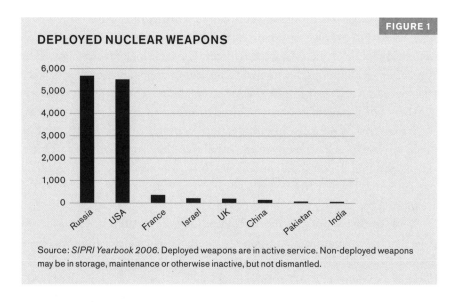

FIGURE 1

DEPLOYED NUCLEAR WEAPONS

Source: *SIPRI Yearbook 2006*. Deployed weapons are in active service. Non-deployed weapons may be in storage, maintenance or otherwise inactive, but not dismantled.

Five states parties to the NPT have nuclear weapons: China, France, Russia, the United Kingdom and the United States. Two non-NPT states, India and Pakistan, have conducted nuclear test explosions and have declared that they possess such weapons. Israel, also a non-NPT party, is generally believed to possess nuclear weapons – by some estimates in the hundreds – although it

---

1. *SIPRI Yearbook 2006*, Appendix 13A, p. 639–668. The SIPRI figures for India, Israel and Pakistan are based on published estimates of the amount of weapon-grade plutonium or highly enriched uranium that these states have allocated to military programmes. Their nuclear arsenals are widely believed to be only partly deployed.

has not officially acknowledged possessing such weapons. North Korea has stated that it possesses nuclear weapons, although estimates vary over the potential size of its arsenal and delivery capabilities.

BOX 3

INDIA-PAKISTAN

India detonated what it called a 'peaceful nuclear device' in 1974. In May 1998, India announced five more nuclear tests and declared that it possessed nuclear weapons. The same month, Pakistan announced six nuclear tests. Neither country has provided many details about the precise yields or designs of such weapons, nor the amount of fissile material each country possesses. Most unofficial estimates claim an arsenal of about 50 weapons for each country. Both state that their weapons are intended for deterrence. India has declared a no-first-use policy, but not Pakistan. Both India and Pakistan support the goal of concluding a multilateral fissile material cut-off treaty, although only Pakistan wants it to cover past production. Both countries are maintaining a moratorium on nuclear testing, but neither has yet signed the CTBT. The Pakistani nuclear scientist A. Q. Khan has been at the centre of illicit international supplier networks involving both imports and exports of nuclear technology and equipment.

The threats posed by existing nuclear weapons relate in the first place to the risks of deliberate use. High representatives of nuclear-armed states have recently alluded in precisely calculated ambiguity to a readiness actually to use nuclear weapons. Additional dangers could arise as a result of accidents, miscalculations, faulty intelligence, theft or unauthorized use. Further threats may arise from the illicit transfer or theft of sensitive design information. As far as the Commission is aware, nuclear weapons have never been stolen or transferred from arsenals of states.

Proliferation

On 31 January 1992, following its first summit meeting, the UN Security Council issued a Presidential Statement declaring that 'the proliferation of all weapons of mass destruction constitutes a threat to international peace and security'. The global proliferation of nuclear weapons actually poses a wide spectrum of threats to regional and global security. These threats multiply as more countries acquire such weapons.

The most fundamental danger is that proliferation will increase the risk of use. As stated in the preamble of the NPT, 'the proliferation of nuclear weapons

BOX 4

THE KOREAN PENINSULA

North Korea has declared that it possesses nuclear weapons, but it has not provided evidence of this claim. It has violated the NPT and twice declared its withdrawal from the treaty. It operates a nuclear fuel cycle consisting of a 5-megawatt research reactor, which uses natural uranium; a reprocessing facility, which produces plutonium; and various uranium processing and fuel fabrication facilities. The United States has claimed that the country also has an enrichment capability. In August 2005, Pakistan's President Musharaff stated that the A. Q. Khan network had provided centrifuge machines and designs to North Korea, although the scale of its enrichment capability remains unknown. North Korea has not signed the Comprehensive Nuclear-Test-Ban Treaty.

would seriously enhance the danger of nuclear war', a theme echoed in many other multilateral accords. The appearance of a new nuclear-weapon programme could have a domino effect, producing fear, alarm and possibly countermeasures involving WMD in neighbouring states.

Even suspicions of such a programme can trigger severe actions, as illustrated by the invasion of Iraq and by the pressures exerted on Iran to refrain from enrichment-related activities.

Weapon designs and related technology can also spread from one country to another, either directly from state to state or through clandestine supplier networks. The most notorious case involved the activities of the Pakistani scientist A.Q. Khan, who was at the centre of two illicit supplier networks – one bringing sensitive technology into Pakistan and another transferring it from Pakistan to Iran, Libya, North Korea and possibly elsewhere. These activities could hardly have taken place without the awareness of the Pakistani government.

The threats and risks described above relate to the geographical – or 'horizontal' – proliferation of WMD. Other risks arise from vertical proliferation, which refers to the expansion or refinement of existing nuclear-weapon capabilities. An endless competition to produce improved weapons fosters new suspicions over military intentions and capabilities. In such a climate, what one state might claim is a prudent safety improvement, another state might view in a more sinister light. Great controversies have arisen in recent years over demands in the United States to develop mini-nukes and bunker busters – initiatives that would be likely to lower the threshold for using nuclear weapons.

BOX 5

WMD THREATS IN THE MIDDLE EAST

Nuclear weapons. Most unofficial estimates claim that *Israel* possesses a nuclear arsenal numbering in the hundreds, possibly larger than the British stockpile. Israel is widely believed to possess both fission and fusion bombs. It has an unsafeguarded plutonium production reactor and reprocessing capability and possibly some uranium enrichment capability, along with various other uranium-processing facilities. It is the only state in the region that is not a party to the NPT. No other state in the region is reported to possess nuclear weapons, although the United States and some other states have claimed that *Iran,* though still only in the early stages of fuel-cycle capability, has a programme to develop such weapons. Iran acquired uranium enrichment technology from Pakistan's A. Q. Khan supplier network and has a uranium enrichment plant under construction, with associated facilities, and a 40-MW heavy water reactor. *Iraq* had for many years a large programme to acquire nuclear weapons; Israel attacked Iraq's Osirak reactor in 1981 and a UN coalition attacked numerous nuclear facilities in 1991; the rest of the nuclear-weapon capability was later destroyed under IAEA supervision. Iraq has not signed the CTBT. *Syria* and *Saudi Arabia* have also not signed the CTBT; neither state has an indigenous infrastructure to support a nuclear-weapons programme. *Egypt, Iran* and *Israel* have signed but not ratified the CTBT.

Biological and chemical weapons. Allegations have been made about both parties and non-parties to the BTWC or the CWC engaging in activities banned by these conventions. *Israel* has not signed the BTWC. It has signed but not ratified the CWC. *Iran* and *Saudi Arabia* are parties to the CWC. *Egypt, Iraq,* and *Syria* have not signed the CWC. *Iraq's* chemical weapons capabilities have been destroyed. *Egypt* and *Syria* have signed but not ratified the BTWC. *Iran, Iraq* and *Saudi Arabia* are parties to the BTWC. *Iraq's* known biological weapons programme was destroyed.

Delivery systems. *Israel* has a significant missile programme – both offensive and defensive, in size as well as in capability. It also has long-range military aircraft with potential WMD delivery capabilities, as do several other countries in the Middle East. *Iran* is developing a series of missiles with ranges over 1,000 kilometres, while *Egypt* and *Syria* have shorter-range missiles. *Saudi Arabia* acquired several intermediate-range missiles (the CSS-2), reportedly about 50, from China in the late 1980s.

Terrorism

For terrorists wishing to develop or acquire nuclear weapons, the greatest difficulty is to obtain weapons-usable fissile material. While there are reports that Pakistani nuclear scientists met with members of al-Qaeda, as far as is known terrorists have not acquired nuclear materials from existing nuclear-weapon arsenals.

It is unlikely that terrorist groups today could develop and manage the substantial infrastructure that would be required to produce enriched uranium or plutonium for weapons. However, nuclear weapons and weapon materials could be stolen by terrorists either from storage or during transportation. Since 1995 the IAEA has maintained an Illicit Trafficking Database, containing (as of December 2004) 662 confirmed incidents of theft, 18 of which involved highly enriched uranium or plutonium, including a few cases involving kilogram quantities.

Much of the US Cooperative Threat Reduction programme is intended to strengthen the physical security of Russia's nuclear weapon-related facilities and weapons-usable nuclear materials, and to reduce the risk that weapon scientists will provide their specialized know-how to terrorists.

Terrorists could also attack nuclear facilities or nuclear materials in transit. This is a serious problem and calls for high standards of physical protection, as discussed in the next chapter.

Terrorist objectives could also be pursued through the use of a so-called dirty bomb, a device designed to disperse radioactive materials. A terrorist group could obtain such materials from nuclear waste or radioactive substances used in hospitals and various industries. Although such weapons are not customarily viewed as WMD because they are not likely to produce very large numbers of fatalities, they are much easier to make than fission weapons and can cause terror and mass disruption, especially if detonated at the heart of major cities.

Biological-weapon threats

Existing weapons

No state acknowledges that it possesses biological weapons or that it has programmes to develop such weapons. Joining a 'biological-weapon club' would not enhance the status of any state. This provides quiet testimony to the enduring strength of both the international stigma attached to them and the fact that they are outlawed by treaty.

A special problem arises from the right affirmed in the BTWC of states to retain biological agents and toxins for prophylactic, protective or other peaceful purposes. In the absence of any verification system this provision, which some have called a loophole in the treaty, makes it difficult for the international community to determine conclusively if a country's declared defensive programmes do not have an offensive military purpose.

Russia and the United States – the countries that once possessed the largest biowarfare programmes – are often cited as retaining various weapon-related capabilities, along with a few other states in the Middle East and East Asia. However, the potential global threat posed by biological weapons is not limited to those states that once had programmes to develop such weapons.

Another problem is that facilities to undertake research on or to produce biological agents are more difficult to detect and easier to hide than facilities to produce fissile material for nuclear weapons. The difficulties of detection enhance the risk of a surprise appearance of a new biological-weapon capability.

Concerns about possible future weapons are even greater than the concerns about today's biological weapons. Studies warn that new biowarfare agents could be developed through genetic engineering and that ways could be explored to weaponize biochemical compounds called bioregulators, which control basic human functions, from thought to action.

Proliferation

The BTWC requires its parties 'not in any way to assist, encourage, or induce any State, group of States or international organization' (Article III) to manufacture biological agents for use as weapons. Regrettably, export controls are not enough to prevent the proliferation of biological weapons. The large biological weapon programme discovered in Iraq, a party to the BTWC, after the 1991 war relied to a large extent on imported agents and growth material. In addition, not only do dangerous biological agents travel internationally unaided by man, they exist in nature inside countries all over the world.

As the scientific, engineering and industrial uses of biological organisms grow throughout the world, states will increasingly be able to produce large volumes of lethal biological agents, engineer new pathogens, and develop effective delivery systems, should they so decide. A related concern is that a state might decide to share its biological-weapon capabilities with a terrorist group.

Terrorism

Experts are divided on the magnitude of the bioterrorist threat. At one extreme, some believe that it may already be, or may soon become, comparable to the threat posed by nuclear weapons. Others are deeply sceptical of the probability of the large-scale use of such weapons by terrorists, given the many technical difficulties of managing such weapons and delivering them effectively.

Non-state actors in the United States used biological agents in 1984, 2001, 2003 and 2004 in local incidents, including some that produced a few fatalities. Other states have had to cope with bioterrorist threats. While none of these incidents resulted in many casualties, the risk will remain in the years ahead that biological or toxin weapons could be used by terrorists.

Expressions of interest by non-state actors in acquiring biological weapons do not prove the existence of a weapon programme, nor do they constitute evidence of a credible capability to deploy such weapons on a large scale. Despite considerable technical and financial resources (reportedly a value of over $1 billion) the Japanese Aum Shinrikyo cult failed in its attempts to use biological weapons on at least ten occasions.

However, past failures by terrorists offer a fragile basis for confident predictions that bioterrorist events will not occur in the future. The bioterrorist threat merits revitalized national and international efforts to prevent such attacks and to substantially improve measures to protect the public against these deadly and indiscriminate weapons.

Chemical-weapon threats

Existing weapons

Historically, the states that produced the most chemical weapons by far were the Soviet Union and the United States (over 40,000 and 30,000 metric tonnes respectively as of 1990). Four other states have declared stocks of chemical weapons. Many experts and government officials have claimed that a number of states, including some that are parties to the CWC, have clandestine chemical-weapon programmes.

As the slow process of verified destruction of chemical weapons continues under the CWC, the threats from remaining stockpiles are gradually receding. Nevertheless, the OPCW reports that, as of 28 February 2006, only 13,049 metric tonnes of chemical agents have been destroyed, of the 71,373 metric tonnes of declared stocks. The individual munitions and containers that have been destroyed represent just over a quarter of the declared items.

Proliferation

While many countries have the capability to make chemical weapons, few countries have the motivation to do so. Such weapons remain repugnant to the overwhelming majority of states and have demonstrated their dubious utility as weapons of war. Nevertheless, the dual-use nature of the commodities and technology that go into the manufacture of chemical weapons remains a persisting concern and a source of uncertainty in any estimates of either arsenal size or latent capabilities to manufacture such weapons.

Terrorism

Toxic chemical agents might be acquired by terrorists through attacks on industries, stocks or shipments. Terrorist groups might also produce such agents themselves. The most notorious case of terrorism involving chemical weapons occurred in 1995, when Aum Shinrikyo used sarin nerve gas in an attack in a Tokyo subway, killing 12 people and sending thousands to hospital. However, as is the case with biological terrorism, delivering toxic materials effectively enough to kill large numbers of people is more difficult than simply acquiring or making the weapon agents.

Rather than seeking to attack large numbers of civilians directly, terrorist groups could choose to attack targets that would release dangerous chemical agents. Civilian industries that use or produce highly toxic materials are sitting targets.

TRADITIONAL RESPONSES TO THREATS OF WEAPONS OF MASS DESTRUCTION

In the light of the variety of motivations and capabilities for acquiring and using WMD, the international community has developed – and is still developing – a range of methods and instruments of response.

While the Commission endorses a wide-ranging response, it views some options advocated as counter-productive and unacceptable – such as the threat of nuclear retaliation against any state or group that might one day use chemical weapons, a stance endorsed by the United States, Russia and, most recently, France. Similarly, the Commission does not endorse the launching of armed interventions that violate the restrictions laid down in the UN Charter.

Instead, the Commission strongly supports the position – often overlooked in discussions on arms control and disarmament – that the first barrier to WMD is a political one. It is the development and maintenance of regional and global peaceful relations. Promoting peace is the prime means of avoiding both the acquisition and the retention of WMD (as well as other weapons). Needless to say, progress in arms control and disarmament will often help to promote peaceful relations. Action against terrorism is similarly in vital need of a political, social dimension in addition to intelligence, policing and military action, which is indispensable as a preventive tool.

States have traditionally sought to reduce or respond to WMD threats by pursuing a wide variety of initiatives, from national to global.

Unilateral responses

Individual countries can initiate measures to reduce WMD threats without requiring any specific quid pro quo. Several examples illustrate how such initiatives have served also to advance international objectives:

- South Africa's decision in 1993 to abandon its nuclear-weapon programme was historic. It demonstrated that a country could indeed walk away from a nuclear-weapon arsenal; that a country could decide on reflection that such weapons were not in its own best security interests; and that it was possible to abandon such a programme, with international verification to check that it truly had.
- Belarus, Kazakhstan and Ukraine also relinquished their physical possession of former Soviet nuclear weapons after the break-up of the USSR.
- Argentina, Brazil, South Korea, Sweden and several other countries unilaterally chose to abandon various nuclear industrial and research pursuits that might have led to nuclear weapons, and they committed themselves to a nuclear-weapon-free status.
- France, Russia, the UK and the US have each unilaterally limited its nuclear arsenal in various ways. As a result of the Presidential Nuclear Initiatives of 1991 and 1992, the United States and Russia unilaterally limited their holdings and deployments of non-strategic nuclear weapons.
- A unilateral presidential decision by the United States to abandon biological weapons substantially facilitated the conclusion of the BTWC.

Although often welcome, unilateral initiatives have limitations. Some of them have not been verified, are not subject to any transparency or reporting requirements, are readily reversible, or are not legally binding. Retiring obsolete weapons while developing replacements cannot be seen as a fulfilment of a commitment to disarm.

Bilateral responses

While states enter into bilateral agreements that serve their interests, other states may also benefit, as may the entire international community. Compliance with bilateral accords is often ensured by the ability of each party directly to respond to any breaches. The parties know that if one withdraws the *quid*, the *quo* may also disappear. Treaties that are open to universal adherence operate somewhat differently. In these, breaches by one party may lead to the reactions of the entire international community, not just of an individual state.

Especially during the Cold War, the United States and the Soviet Union found it in their mutual interest to reach agreements to limit their nuclear weapons and missile capabilities and otherwise work to reduce the risk of global nuclear war. These agreements, and later Russian-US agreements that are also in the interest of the international community, include:

- the 1963 Hotline Agreement;
- the Strategic Arms Limitation Treaties (the 1972 SALT I and 1979 SALT II treaties), and the Anti-Ballistic Missile (ABM) Treaty, also signed in 1972;
- the 1987 Treaty on the Elimination of Intermediate-Range and Shorter-Range Missiles (INF Treaty);
- the Strategic Arms Reduction Treaties (the 1991 START I and 1993 START II treaties);
- the framework agreement announced at the Clinton-Yeltsin summit in Helsinki in March 1997, which set forth terms for a START III treaty and clarified key constraints in the ABM Treaty;
- the 2002 Strategic Offensive Reductions Treaty (Moscow Treaty).

Just as such bilateral agreements may serve broader international security interests, their breakdown can produce the opposite result. The United States unilaterally withdrew from the ABM Treaty in 2002. Three years later, a senior US official testified in Congress that one of the reasons why China was 'modernizing and expanding its ballistic missile forces' was to 'overcome ballistic missile defence systems'.[2] Following this withdrawal, President Putin announced that Russia was no longer bound by the START II Treaty. Plans for implementing the 1997 framework agreement for START III have been killed, and the 1997 joint statement on the ABM Treaty is now irrelevant.

---

2. Vice Admiral Lowell E. Jacoby, Director of the Defense Intelligence Agency, Statement for the Record, 'Current and Projected National Security Threats', Senate Select Committee on Intelligence, 16 February 2005, p. 11.

Bilateral agreements and understandings have also been used to reduce nuclear concerns between Argentina and Brazil (1990) and India and Pakistan (1988). In the former case, Argentina and Brazil agreed to cooperate in the peaceful uses of nuclear energy and to renounce nuclear weapons, while in the latter, India and Pakistan agreed not to attack each other's nuclear facilities. In February 1999, India and Pakistan also signed a memorandum of understanding on a variety of nuclear confidence-building measures. Both countries, however, are continuing their efforts to develop and produce nuclear weapons and their delivery vehicles.

Plurilateral responses

Activities undertaken by more than two parties, but not involving all states in a region or all members of the international community, might be termed plurilateral. Such initiatives often relate to specific controversies or to export control arrangements.

In 2003 Libya announced that it would abandon all its WMD programmes. Although the decision was Libya's, it came after long negotiations, notably with the UK and the US. It may be said to have constituted a successful example of a plurilateral effort.

China, Japan, North Korea, Russia, South Korea and the United States have been engaged in six-party talks aimed at eliminating North Korea's nuclear-weapon programme and promoting peace on the Korean peninsula. This plurilateral action is further discussed in Chapter 3.

In another initiative, France, Germany and the UK – with EU support – have been actively engaged in talks with Iran to address continuing concerns, especially over activities related to the enrichment of uranium in Iran. While not participating directly in the initiative, the United States, Russia and China have been engaged in offering proposals intended to facilitate a solution to the issues. This question is also further treated in Chapter 3.

The initiative of the Group of Eight major industrialized countries (G8) known as the Global Partnership against the Spread of Weapons and Materials of Mass Destruction may also be seen as a plurilateral initiative. It relies on relatively traditional methods to reduce the risk of proliferation of WMD and promote disarmament. This initiative was launched in 2002 at a meeting of the G8 countries (Canada, France, Germany, Italy, Japan, Russia, the United Kingdom and the United States), and featured a collective commitment to invest some $20 billion over a decade. Focusing initially on Russia, it has provided technical assistance, equipment and training to address WMD issues.

Other plurilateral actions seek to establish common understandings among groups of states about the design and operation of export controls to impede the proliferation of WMD – the Nuclear Suppliers Group, the Australia Group and the Missile Technology Control Regime. Export controls are discussed in Chapter 7.

Regional responses

Sometimes states in a given region join in initiatives against WMD threats.

The European Union, for example, is pursuing several initiatives to strengthen its cooperation to reduce the threat of WMD. In 2003, it adopted a Strategy against the Proliferation of Weapons of Mass Destruction. It is based on the premise *inter alia* that the best solution to the problem of proliferation of WMD is to convince countries that they do not need them. It urges 'effective multilateralism', including export controls. It envisions, when other measures have failed, the possible use of coercive measures under Chapter VII of the UN Charter, with the Security Council playing a central role.

Other significant regional measures include treaties establishing nuclear-weapon-free zones (NWFZ) in Latin America, the South Pacific, Africa and Southeast Asia. Together, these initiatives have excluded the stationing of nuclear weapons on virtually all territories south of the equator. Efforts are under way to establish a NWFZ in Central Asia.

States which agree that their region should forgo WMD are motivated by an interest in ensuring that all states in their own neighbourhood will not possess WMD. (This is particularly clear in the Tlatelolco Treaty, which provided that it would not enter into force for individual countries until all countries in Latin America and the Caribbean had ratified it.)

The establishment of a zone free of all WMD in the Middle East has long been supported by all the states in the region, although the continuation of the conflict has made this impossible. A WMD-free zone in the Middle East may eventually help all the states in the region to satisfy their security interests. One state's renunciation of WMD can be linked to and made dependent upon a defined group of other states (including Israel and Iran) doing the same. The arrangement's reliability may be enhanced by the awareness of all that any breach may lead to the collapse of the whole agreement. For the stability and reliability of such arrangements, all parties are likely to demand both international and some form of mutual verification, and perhaps some guarantees by outside powers.

In the next chapter, the Commission develops the thought that some steps towards creating such a zone could be taken even now as a part of the Middle East peace process.

Global responses

Among the traditional responses to the threats of WMD, the global conventions described in the beginning of this report are the most central and the most important: the NPT, the BTWC and the CWC.

Like many conventions on human rights and the Geneva Conventions, these three instruments are as close as the international community has come so far to enacting legislation. There are important differences, however: while the international community aspires for universal acceptance and respect for the rules of conventions, adherence is voluntary, withdrawal is not excluded and the enforcement of rules is not guaranteed.

Nevertheless, the obligations assumed by each state party to any one of these conventions are not linked directly to the identical individual obligation assumed by other parties. The treaties are intended to protect and promote interests that the parties have in common and to do so regardless of whether all states join and apply the rules. A breach of a rule by one party may not lead to counter-measures by other parties. To take an example: the violation of the CWC by one country does not oblige other states parties to respond. However, the breach might weaken other countries' loyalty to and their political support for the treaty and thus erode its effectiveness. On the other hand, such a breach might lead to a collective response by other countries that decide, as stakeholders, to take a stand.

Another example is the NPT. It contains no *quid pro quos* between the parties. However, it does require all non-nuclear-weapon states parties to forgo nuclear weapons, and all parties, notably the five nuclear-weapon states, to both pursue global nuclear disarmament and facilitate the peaceful uses of atomic energy. Non-compliance with any of these obligations might trigger withdrawals, might lead to collective reactions or might simply weaken the glue that holds the parties together in the treaty. Compliance by Iraq, Libya and Iran in today's uncertain atmosphere is important to all. So is compliance by the nuclear-weapon states. They need to uphold the commitments they made at the 1995 NPT Review and Extension Conference to secure the extension of the treaty – and consequently also the thirteen steps agreed at the 2000 NPT Review Conference in order to implement the 1995 agreements.

BOX 6

SUMMARY OF THE THIRTEEN PRACTICAL STEPS
FOR NUCLEAR DISARMAMENT AGREED IN 2000

1. Early entry into force of the CTBT.
2. A moratorium on nuclear tests pending the CTBT's entry into force.
3. Conclude negotiations in the CD on a verifiable fissile materials treaty within five years.
4. Establish a subsidiary body in the CD to deal with nuclear disarmament.
5. Apply the principle of irreversibility nuclear disarmament and arms control.
6. An unequivocal undertaking by the nuclear-weapon states (NWS) to eliminate their nuclear arsenals.
7. Entry into force of START II; conclusion of START III; preserve the ABM Treaty.
8. Completion and implementation of the Trilateral Initiative.
9. Steps by the nuclear-weapon states leading to nuclear disarmament in a way that promotes international stability, based on the principle of undiminished security for all:
    *   Unilateral reductions;
    *   Increased transparency;
    *   The further reduction of non-strategic nuclear weapons;
    *   De-alerting;
    *   A diminishing role for nuclear weapons in security policies;
    *   The engagement by all the nuclear-weapon states in disarmament as soon as appropriate.
10. Arrangements by nuclear-weapon states to place fissile material no longer required for military purposes under IAEA supervision or other relevant international verification.
11. Reaffirmation that the ultimate objective is general and complete disarmament under effective international control.
12. Regular reports within the NPT's strengthened review process.
13. Improved verification of compliance with nuclear disarmament agreements.

Other relevant global instruments that still remain to be completed or brought into force include:

■ The Comprehensive Nuclear-Test-Ban Treaty (CTBT) – which has been ratified by 132 states (as of April 2006), but has not yet entered into force.

■ A fissile materials cut-off treaty (FMCT) – which has widespread support but has not yet been negotiated.

- A global treaty assuring non-nuclear-weapon states against threats of attack with nuclear weapons (negative security assurances).
- A global treaty outlawing the weaponization of outer space.

WEAKNESSES IN TRADITIONAL RESPONSES

The traditional cooperative approach to tackling the threats of WMD, in particular the reliance on global conventions, has been the subject of criticism, some unjustified, some fair. Obviously, during the life of a treaty problems may arise that did not exist at the time when they were drafted. However, treaties are not necessarily frozen in time. It is the task of review conferences to identify new problems and seek solutions to them. New arrangements, amendments or additional agreements may be devised that address the unforeseen problems while preserving the consensus that was the basis of the treaty. Yet, several weaknesses of the traditional approaches persist. They are discussed below.

Lack of universality

Given the strength resulting from universal – or nearly universal – adherence to binding treaty regimes, the world community has made, and must continue to make, energetic efforts to promote this goal with respect to several arms control and disarmament treaties.

In the case of the NPT, the licence given to the P5 and the non-adherence of India, Israel and Pakistan constitute real limitations on the central aims of the treaty. Non-membership of the BTWC and the CWC, however, may often be due less to any substantive objection to the goal of eliminating such weapons than to other issues. Some states have not viewed joining these treaties as a matter of urgency. Others, some of which may possess chemical and/or biological weapons, appear to link their future participation in these treaties to progress in inducing Israel to join the NPT.

In the case of the CTBT, the legal ban on nuclear test explosions has not materialized because of the absence of the US and a number of other ratifications required for its entry into force.

The problem of unmet requirements for entry into force has also arisen in some regional arrangements. For instance, the Pelindaba Treaty, establishing a nuclear-weapon-free zone in Africa, although signed in 1996 has still not entered into force because of an insufficient number of ratifications.

Withdrawal

An important limitation in various arms control and disarmament treaties is that they allow for the possibility of states to withdraw. The three global WMD treaties all contain provisions allowing states to withdraw under the particular circumstance of supreme national interest, subject to a requirement to provide some advance notice. (See Box 7.) After North Korea's decision to withdraw from the NPT, this right has been criticized.

The Commission doubts that it would be either possible or desirable to seek to eliminate the right of withdrawal from the NPT or other WMD treaties. States view the right of withdrawal as a matter that may affect their security and bears directly on their sovereignty. Without this right they might not have joined the treaty, and eliminating it could serve to discourage additional states from joining.

However, it could reasonably be made more difficult to withdraw. Many would like to see a way of exerting pressure on states that appear intent on terminating their WMD commitments. Several proposals with various options have been made by Germany, the European Union and others, including the following:

- Establishing a requirement for a special conference of the state parties upon the announcement of intent to withdraw.
- Agreeing at a treaty review conference on an interpretative statement of the method for implementing a withdrawal.
- Obliging any state that implements a withdrawal to forfeit the right to retain or to use any of the technology or goods it acquired as a treaty party.

Regardless of whether such proposals are implemented, any withdrawal must – as provided in the three multilateral WMD treaties – come to the attention of the Security Council. The Council can then examine whether any planned withdrawal constitutes a threat to the peace and can consider what measures it might wish to take in response.

Inadequate verification

In Chapter 8 of this report, the Commission makes the case that international verification is a vital element for creating confidence in compliance with arms control and disarmament treaties. Verification provides vital means for both deterring and discovering breaches and provides a factual basis for determining what the reaction against such breaches should be. While IAEA safeguards inspections revealed that declarations by North Korea regarding its

BOX 7

TREATY WITHDRAWAL:
NOTIFICATION REQUIREMENTS
(Italics added)

Non-Proliferation Treaty

Article X

1. Each Party shall in exercising its national sovereignty have the right to withdraw from the Treaty if it decides that extraordinary events, related to the subject matter of this Treaty, have jeopardized the supreme interests of its country. *It shall give notice of such withdrawal to all other Parties to the Treaty and to the United Nations Security Council three months in advance.* Such notice shall include a statement of the extraordinary events it regards as having jeopardized its supreme interests.

Biological and Toxin Weapons Convention

Article XIII

(1) This Convention shall be of unlimited duration.

(2) Each State Party to this Convention shall in exercising its natural sovereignty have the right to withdraw from the Convention if it decides that extraordinary events, related to the subject matter of the Convention, have jeopardized the supreme interests of its country. *It shall give notice of such withdrawal to all other States Parties to the Convention and to the United Nations Security Council three months in advance.* Such notice shall include a statement of the extraordinary events it regards as having jeopardized its supreme interests.

Chemical Weapons Convention

Article XVI
DURATION AND WITHDRAWAL

2. Each State Party shall, in exercising its national sovereignty, have the right to withdraw from this Convention if it decides that extraordinary events, related to the subject-matter of this Convention, have jeopardized the supreme interests of its country. *It shall give notice of such withdrawal 90 days in advance to all other States Parties, the Executive Council, the Depositary and the United Nations Security Council.* Such notice shall include a statement of the extraordinary events it regards as having jeopardized its supreme interests.

holdings of plutonium were misleading, they failed to discover the efforts of Iraq and Libya to develop nuclear weapons. They also did not discover the failure of Iran to respect all its safeguards obligations.

These experiences led governments to the conclusion that the traditional kind of nuclear safeguards verification, which had been developed and accepted in the 1960s, did not have the necessary teeth and needed to be strengthened to serve the present needs of the nuclear non-proliferation regime.

Detection techniques have developed significantly in recent years. Improved safeguards standards were adopted by the IAEA in 1997, known as the Additional Protocol. As of 13 March 2006, Additional Protocols were in force in 75 NPT states. Although even the improved safeguards can hardly give 100% confidence about compliance – it is rarely possible to prove a negative – they mark a leap forward. They must become the accepted minimum standard for all inspections under the NPT. National surveillance systems may supplement international verification but, as experience has repeatedly shown, particularly with Iraq, such systems do not offer a panacea.

In the case of bioweapons, there is no verification regime for the BTWC. The confidence-building measures that are in place are only voluntary. For the CWC, its highly elaborate verification regime has been limited by at least one state's refusal to allow the most intrusive type of inspections. If one or more states do not allow these important tools to be used, other states will also refuse.

Non-compliance

The vast majority of states parties to the key WMD treaties are complying with their obligations under the treaties, and the regimes contribute in an important way to stability and confidence. Nevertheless, the many years of undiscovered non-compliance with the BTWC by the Soviet Union and later Iraq took a toll on that treaty. The NPT violations by Iraq, Libya and North Korea resulted in a severe loss of confidence in the effectiveness of the treaty. While Iran has adamantly denied that it is seeking to acquire nuclear weapons, its breaches of its safeguards obligations have also raised questions about its long-term intentions.

The erosion of confidence in the effectiveness of the NPT to prevent horizontal proliferation has been matched by a loss of confidence in the treaty as a result of the failure of the nuclear-weapon states to fulfil their disarmament obligations under the treaty and also to honour their additional commitments to disarmament made at the 1995 and 2000 NPT Review Conferences.

Lack of enforcement

Monitoring and verification are instruments to create confidence in states' compliance by detecting possible violations of their WMD commitments. Yet, apart from referring specific cases to the UN Security Council and action by the Council, there are few institutional measures to enforce any of these treaties. (However, the executive boards of both the IAEA and the OPCW may consider responding by the withdrawal of technical assistance or the suspension of membership.) It is appropriate to note that there is no enforcement of the nuclear-weapon states' disarmament commitments under the NPT. Like the violations of the non-proliferation pledge, their failure simply results in a degree of erosion of support for the treaty.

There are also some significant limitations in the ability of the various plurilateral regimes (the Nuclear Suppliers Group, the Australia Group, the Missile Technology Control Regime and the Hague Code of Conduct) to ensure export controls relating to non-proliferation worldwide. There is by no means universal participation in these regimes, but it is growing. When suppliers of sensitive items do not participate, this substantially hinders enforcement.

NEW RESPONSES TO THREATS FROM WEAPONS OF TERROR

The weaknesses and difficulties of traditional cooperative approaches to arms control and disarmament may have contributed to some scepticism of the treaty regimes – even a shift of approach – on the part of some policy makers. This is especially true of the United States. To the extent new initiatives regarding WMD have been proposed, they have tended to focus on issues pertaining to specific countries, including Iran, Iraq, Libya and North Korea or on initiatives against terrorist threats.

Moreover, this change has led to a reduced reliance on global institutions and instruments and a greater emphasis on new approaches comprising unilateral and plurilateral action, including ad hoc 'coalitions of the willing' and the use of more coercive measures. While some measures have been welcomed as serving the common goals of the WMD treaties, others have been fiercely criticized.

The 2003 Proliferation Security Initiative (PSI) represents a new approach that has met with support but also some scepticism. It was launched by the United States, which gathered a coalition of states that have agreed to use their national resources, including force if necessary, to interdict and seize international shipments of goods believed to be illegally destined for use in WMD programmes. Currently, the PSI is targeted at an undisclosed set of 'states or non-state actors of proliferation concern'.

While the number of states participating in the PSI has expanded considerably since 2003, the initiative has also generated criticism over issues relating to its consistency with international law, its lack of transparency and other concerns. The Commission discusses this initiative in its treatment in Chapter 7 of the controls over the movement of goods.

UN Security Council Resolution 1540 (April 2004) represents another new approach and significant recent development. It establishes a mandatory requirement for all states to refrain from providing any form of support to non-state actors in obtaining WMD. It also mandates them to adopt domestic legislation to implement this obligation. More broadly and importantly, it requires states to establish national controls to prevent the proliferation of WMD and their means of delivery.

Given the uneven track record of states in implementing international obligations to prevent terrorism or WMD proliferation, such a resolution is welcome. It urges states to 'renew and fulfil their commitment to multilateral cooperation'. It thus helps to solidify the foundation of traditional cooperation, while also expanding the scope of many WMD-related obligations to non-parties to the WMD regimes and the several conventions against terrorism. If the Security Council provides the necessary institutional resources for monitoring the implementation of the resolution and assists states in complying, this would seem to have significant potential.

As discussed in Chapter 8, Resolution 1540 illustrates the potential of the UN Security Council to bring about rules that are mandatory for the entire world community. The Security Council is the only institution in the world that has the legal authority to examine – and if need be harmonize, supplement and enforce – the many efforts made to counter and reduce the threats posed by WMD. However, this responsibility, if it is to be accepted by the world community of nations, must be exercised not by a small group dominated by five great powers but in broad consultation with and for the benefit of the whole UN membership.

Counter-proliferation

Counter-proliferation as a means of combating WMD is not entirely new. Israel bombed Iraq's Osirak reactor in 1981 in order to slow down or prevent Iraq's nuclear-weapon programme. Counter-proliferation has been a part of

US policy for some time. It comprises many different elements, including some that are welcome, like the US Cooperative Threat Reduction programme. However, it also comprises the readiness to use armed force to prevent or impede the proliferation of WMD, in cases deemed to constitute 'growing threats' to the US. While it may be assumed that the US prefers to obtain support for such a use of force through the endorsement of the Security Council, an endorsement is not regarded as essential even in actions that cannot plausibly be described as self-defence and therefore permitted under Article 51 of the UN Charter.

States with sufficient military power may decide to take unilateral armed action against states with weapons or programmes of WMD believed to pose a threat. It is an entirely different matter for the community of states to recognize such action as legal and legitimate. The case of Iraq demonstrates that a large number of UN members, including allies of the US, will only accept as legal unilateral armed action in self-defence against armed attacks when they are actually under way, or imminent. Where there is no imminence, there is time, they believe, to submit the threat to the Security Council for it to judge the evidence and authorize – or not to authorize – armed action or decide on other measures. The Commission shares this view.

THREE CONCLUSIONS FOR COLLECTIVE ACTION

It is clear from the above that a lowering of the WMD threat requires many parallel and reinforcing approaches in the fields of arms control, disarmament, non-proliferation and anti-terrorism, at all levels – unilateral, bilateral, regional, plurilateral and global. Progress has been made over time and further progress is perfectly possible. Shortcomings in existing rules and regimes can be easily identified – in verification, compliance and enforcement. They can and must be remedied. Gaps must be filled and what is broken must be fixed. This should be done, however, without breaking the consensus that brought the rules and regimes into being – above all, the basic bargain between nuclear non-proliferation and disarmament. While leadership and initiative by individual nations, including the great powers, have much to contribute in the efforts to counter WMD, all states are stakeholders and must be included in the effort. Just as peace and order in a nation are best maintained if the consent and participation of its citizens are secured, international progress towards peace, order and the reduction of arms, including WMD, can best be attained through the participation and cooperation of all governments and peoples.

The Commission concludes accordingly that:

- There is a need to revitalize and strengthen *multilateral cooperative* approaches, because of both their legitimacy and their potential effectiveness in addressing WMD threats.
- There is a need to re-instil a sense of *collective responsibility* among governments for achieving the disarmament, non-proliferation and counter-terrorism goals which their official policies nominally support.
- The Security Council – in close contact with the members of the UN – should be the *focal point* for the world's efforts to reduce the threats posed by existing and future WMD, and to help harmonize, supplement and enforce the many efforts that are made.

Nuclear weapons

CHAPTER 3

Nuclear weapons

So long as any state has nuclear weapons, others will want them. So long as any such weapons remain, there is a risk that they will one day be used, by design or accident. And any such use would be catastrophic.

The accumulated threat posed by the estimated 27,000 nuclear weapons, in Russia, the United States and the other NPT nuclear-weapon states, merits worldwide concern. However, especially in these five states the view is common that nuclear weapons from the first wave of proliferation somehow are tolerable, while such weapons in the hands of additional states are viewed as dangerous.

In this view, the second wave of proliferation, which added Israel, India and Pakistan, was unwelcome – the lack of political stability in Pakistan being a special source of concern. However, efforts to induce these states to roll back their programmes – as South Africa did – have gradually been weakened and are now largely abandoned. As none of them was a party to the NPT, they could not be charged with a violation of the treaty.

The third wave of proliferation, consisting of Iraq, Libya, North Korea and possibly Iran, is seen as a mortal danger and has met with a much more forceful reaction.

The Commission rejects the suggestion that nuclear weapons in the hands of some pose no threat, while in the hands of others they place the world in mortal jeopardy. Governments possessing nuclear weapons can act responsibly or recklessly. Governments may also change over time. Twenty-seven thousand nuclear weapons are not an abstract theory. They exist in today's world. The Hiroshima and Nagasaki bombs, each of which had an explosive yield of less than 20 kilotons of TNT, killed some 200,000 people. The W-76 – the standard nuclear warhead used on US Trident submarine-launched ballistic missiles – has a yield of up to 100 kilotons. During the Cold War, the Soviet Union manufactured and tested nuclear weapons with yields of over 50 megatons of TNT.

The questions of how to reduce the threat and the number of existing nuclear weapons must be addressed with no less vigour than the question of the threat from additional weapons, whether in the hands of existing nuclear-weapon states, proliferating states or terrorists.

It is probably true that an agreement by all nuclear-armed states to, say, a fissile material cut-off would not in itself prevent the proliferation threat posed by North Korea or Iran. Nevertheless, dissuading potential proliferators from moving further along the path of nuclear-weapon development, and maintaining support by the global community for non-proliferation, is made more difficult when the nuclear-weapon states make little effort to achieve nuclear disarmament. Explanations by the nuclear-haves that the weapons are indispensable to defend their sovereignty are not the best way to convince other sovereign states to renounce the option. The single most hopeful step to revitalize non-proliferation and disarmament today would be ratification of the CTBT by all states that have nuclear weapons.

As was seen in 2005, both at the NPT Review Conference and at the United Nations World Summit, the world community will not agree to choose between non-proliferation and disarmament. This chapter advances recommendations on both fronts.

BOX 8

SOME PROGRESS IN REDUCING NUCLEAR THREATS

- The non-use of nuclear weapons since 1945 shows that there is a significant threshold against use.
- Nearly all states in the world have adhered to the NPT, including four states that have been in possession of nuclear weapons – South Africa and three former members of the Soviet Union. With a few notable exceptions the parties are abiding by their commitment not to acquire nuclear weapons.
- Regional nuclear-weapon-free zones have made virtually the entire southern hemisphere off-limits for the stationing of nuclear weapons. Other treaties outlaw basing such weapons on the seabed, in outer space and in Antarctica.
- The Partial Test-Ban Treaty bans nuclear testing everywhere except underground. While the Comprehensive Nuclear-Test-Ban Treaty has not entered into force, a moratorium against testing is being upheld.
- The US and Russia have withdrawn thousands of nuclear weapons from service. The UK has significantly reduced its arsenal after the end of the Cold War, while France no longer deploys nuclear weapons on surface-to-surface missiles or as gravity bombs.

Over the six decades following the attacks on Hiroshima and Nagasaki, numerous initiatives have been launched to control and eliminate nuclear weapons and to prevent proliferation. They have had mixed results. Seen from one perspective, the efforts have failed. At least eight and possibly nine states have acquired nuclear weapons. Global stocks of these weapons are still huge, and more states and even terrorists might acquire them. But against this there have been some positive achievements (see Box 8).

The three major challenges the world confronts – existing weapons, further proliferation and terrorism – are interlinked politically, and also practically: the larger the existing stocks, the greater the danger of leakage and misuse. This chapter begins by addressing the proliferation issue because it has been at the forefront of international debate and action in recent years. But the Commission takes all three challenges equally seriously. Progress and innovative solutions are needed on all fronts.

PREVENTING THE PROLIFERATION OF NUCLEAR WEAPONS

The Non-Proliferation Treaty

Having entered into force in 1970, the NPT is the cornerstone of the global non-proliferation regime. The original 'bargain' of the treaty is generally understood to be the elimination of nuclear weapons through the commitment by non-nuclear-weapon states not to acquire nuclear weapons and the commitment by five nuclear-weapon states to pursue nuclear disarmament. In addition, the treaty requires parties to facilitate peaceful uses of nuclear energy through exchanges of various kinds between themselves. They also promise to enter into safeguards agreements with the IAEA and to exercise control over their national nuclear-related exports. Only four countries in the world (India, Israel, North Korea and Pakistan) are not parties to the treaty. What accounts for this near universality?

Many states did not perceive a need for nuclear weapons of their own. Some had assurances of protection through their alliances and other arrangements. Some may well have responded to political and diplomatic pressure to renounce nuclear weapons, while others may not have had a technical capability to develop them. Yet others, even if they could have made a nuclear weapon, have abhorred such weapons and wanted to join a treaty that could be an obstacle to the continued possession of the deadliest weapon in history.

Conversely, when states have perceived threats to their security (like

India, Israel, Pakistan and South Africa) or have felt ostracized and at risk (like North Korea, Libya and Iran), this may have weighed heavily in their calculations. In Iraq's case, by contrast, Saddam Hussein's efforts to develop nuclear weapons may have been motivated more by a wish to dominate and expand Iraq's influence in the region than by concerns about national security.

The two basic ideas at the heart of the NPT continue to have strong international support – that more fingers on more nuclear triggers would result in a more dangerous world, and that non-proliferation by the have-nots and disarmament by the haves will together lead to a safer world. Nevertheless, the fact that the treaty is facing several problems must be squarely faced.

The first problem relates to the *failure to make progress towards nuclear disarmament* by the nuclear-weapon states parties.

The second set of problems concerns the *breaches of the treaty or of IAEA safeguards obligations* by a small number of parties: Iraq, Libya, North Korea and Iran. Their actions have undermined the confidence in the NPT. A domino effect, it has been suggested, may lead more countries to acquire nuclear weapons. However, while it is necessary to examine the fundamental questions of verification, compliance, reliability and enforcement, one must note that the world is not replete with would-be proliferators nor, as yet, with nuclear-capable terrorists. As long as relations between the great powers are characterized by cooperation and regional tensions are not heightened, there is probably little reason to fear a collapse of the NPT.

A third problem, related to the second and illustrated by the case of North Korea, is that the treaty's provision regarding *withdrawal* fails to identify such action as the serious event it is. It makes it simply procedural. As indicated in Chapter 2, any notice of withdrawal must be brought to the attention of all other states parties and the UN Security Council, which will examine whether the planned withdrawal constitutes a threat to the peace and consider what measures it might take. If the Security Council fails to respond to a withdrawal, other parties might later decide to reconsider their own continued adherence to the treaty.

A fourth problem may be characterized as *technical*. The lack of any provision for a standing secretariat to assist the parties in implementing the treaty has proven inconvenient.

In fact, the NPT is the weakest of the treaties on WMD in terms of provisions about implementation. The IAEA and its Board of Governors are not the secretariat of the treaty, and the three depositary governments – the Russian, the British and the US – have only been given the formal task of convoking review conferences. The NPT has no provisions for consultations or special meetings of the parties to consider cases of possible non-compliance or withdrawal, nor to assist in the implementation of the treaty between the five-yearly Review Conferences. The governments of Canada, Ireland and many other states have offered constructive proposals to address this institutional deficit, with options that include creating a standing bureau or executive committee of the parties. Yet the problem persists, and the periodic meetings of the treaty review process cannot offer an effective substitute for this needed institutional reform.

The problems described above do not diminish the fundamental support for the treaty but there is unquestionably a serious malaise among parties, as shown in their inability to adopt any common conclusions at the 2005 Review Conference.

The hope and expectation have faded – at least for now – that the basic bargain of the treaty between nuclear-weapon and non-nuclear-weapon states should lead to parallel and mutually reinforcing processes of non-proliferation and disarmament. There is a background to this concern.

Evolving treaty commitments

The negotiation of the NPT in the late 1960s was not as easy as might be assumed. Several non-nuclear-weapon states were critical of the imbalance between the precise obligations of the non-nuclear-weapon states and the imprecise commitments of the nuclear powers. One result was a provision stating that the treaty would remain in force for only 25 years, requiring a subsequent decision on an extension.

During the 1970s and 1980s, the failure of the nuclear-weapon states to make progress on disarmament and to halt nuclear testing led to growing criticism from the non-nuclear-weapon states. Many states, not only in the Middle East, voiced their concern that Israel remained outside the treaty while other states in the region were subject to NPT constraints. The indefinite extension of the NPT in 1995 was not a forgone conclusion.

While the parties ultimately agreed in 1995, after intensive negotiations, to extend the treaty indefinitely, this decision was adopted only as part of a package of commitments. This included a decision on principles and objectives for non-proliferation and disarmament, a decision on strengthening the treaty review process and a resolution on the establishment of a WMD-free zone in the Middle East. The disarmament goals called for completion of a CTBT, negotiations on a verifiable fissile material cut-off treaty, and further systematic progress on reducing and eliminating nuclear weapons. The parties showed that it was possible to reconcile their strong and diverse individual interests.

The treaty's 2000 Review Conference carried on this process of multilateral cooperation. It agreed on a Final Document that included 'the thirteen practical steps' for further progress towards nuclear disarmament. These were seen as representing a continuation and development of the agreements that had secured the indefinite extension of the NPT five years earlier.

At the 2005 Review Conference this cooperative approach was missing. The conference ended in acrimony and without any final statement. 'The thirteen practical steps' (see Box 6) were played down by the nuclear-weapon states and not recognized as important commitments. The inability of the World Summit in September 2005 to adopt any statement about disarmament and non-proliferation was caused by a renewed failure to balance commitments in the two areas. The obvious question therefore is: what can be done to revitalize the NPT?

WMDC RECOMMENDATION

1 All parties to the Non-Proliferation Treaty need to revert to the fundamental and balanced non-proliferation and disarmament commitments that were made under the treaty and confirmed in 1995 when the treaty was extended indefinitely.

WMDC RECOMMENDATION

2 All parties to the Non-Proliferation Treaty should implement the decision on principles and objectives for non-proliferation and disarmament, the decision on strengthening the Non-Proliferation Treaty review process, and the resolution on the Middle East as a zone free of nuclear and all other weapons of mass destruction, all adopted in 1995. They should also promote the implementation of 'the thirteen practical steps' for nuclear disarmament that were adopted in 2000.

WMDC RECOMMENDATION

3 To enhance the effectiveness of the nuclear non-proliferation regime, all Non-Proliferation Treaty non-nuclear-weapon states parties should accept comprehensive safeguards as strengthened by the International Atomic Energy Agency Additional Protocol.

WMDC RECOMMENDATION

The states parties to the Non-Proliferation Treaty should establish a standing secretariat to handle administrative matters for the parties to the treaty. This secretariat should organize the treaty's Review Conferences and their Preparatory Committee sessions. It should also organize other treaty-related meetings upon the request of a majority of the states parties.

Cases of non-compliance

In the introduction to this chapter, three cases of breach and one case of possible breach of the NPT were mentioned: Iraq, Libya, North Korea and Iran.

The first two cases are now history: that of Libya was discovered through intelligence and solved through diplomacy, supported by pressure. The breach by Iraq was discovered during the war of 1991 and eliminated as a result of the subsequent sanctions and inspections instituted by the UN and supported by political and military pressure.

Lessons can be learned from these two cases. It could be a good idea to draw up procedures that would be automatically applicable in the case of breaches of the NPT. The general question of enforcement is discussed in Chapter 8. Here, it may suffice to note that there are considerable variations in non-compliance situations, calling for very different responses. To intervene against states is not quite the same as intervening against individuals. The present intervention by armed force in Iraq is extremely costly in terms of human lives, suffering and the destruction of economic resources. In the case of Libya, diplomacy – supported by the pressure of the UN and the threat of the possible use of force – proved to be effective. In the event of future breaches of the NPT, including significant breaches of safeguards obligations, pressures will grow among parties for such matters to be brought to the attention of the Security Council, and rightly so. While the Council's response will depend upon the circumstances of the specific case, a record of failing to respond would have implications well beyond the treaty.

In addressing the cases of North Korea and Iran, it is clear that *security* factors are of particular significance. In many cases, perceived threats to security have been the incentive for the acquisition of nuclear weapons and security guarantees of various kinds have offered disincentives. It is not unreasonable to think that the governments of Libya, Iran and North Korea, often isolated, have convinced themselves that their security was threatened. In the case of Iran there was also a very real threat from Iraq, which armed itself with WMD and used chemical weapons against Iran during the long war of the 1980s. It is possible that in such states incentives to acquire nuclear weapons may be reduced by offers of normal relations and by assurances that military intervention or subversion aiming at regime change will not be undertaken.

North Korea acceded to the NPT in 1985, a decade after South Korea joined. In 1992, North Korea's long-delayed safeguards agreement with the IAEA entered into force and IAEA inspections started. The same year North and South Korea signed a Joint Declaration on the Denuclearization of the Korean Peninsula. In that accord the parties agreed, *inter alia*, not to develop, test or acquire nuclear weapons and not to possess nuclear reprocessing or uranium enrichment facilities (as these are needed for the production of weapons-usable plutonium and enriched uranium).

It was not long before IAEA safeguards inspections showed that North Korea must have produced more plutonium than it had declared. This was reported to the Agency Board of Governors, which referred the case as a breach of safeguards obligations to the Security Council. North Korea declared that it intended to withdraw from the NPT, while the Council contented itself with a brief resolution in which UN member states were urged to take steps to promote a solution.

After negotiations between the United States and North Korea an Agreed Framework was drawn up in 1994. Under this document North Korea declared that it would freeze its existing nuclear programme, accept inspections by the IAEA, rejoin the NPT, implement the agreement on the denuclearization of the Korean peninsula and eventually dismantle its nuclear plants. The US would help to arrange the financing and supply of two 1,000-MW(e) nuclear light-water reactors and the supply of heavy oil. Both nations would ease trade restrictions and move towards diplomatic relations. The US would provide formal assurance against the threat or use of nuclear weapons.

After a long process during which the Agreed Framework eroded – with each side blaming the other for defaults – new talks were instituted in August 2003 with a six-party group consisting of China, Japan, North Korea, Russia, South Korea and the United States attempting to reconstitute the previous détente.

By February 2005, however, the US was convinced that North Korea was developing a capability to enrich uranium based on technology obtained secretly through the international network of Pakistani scientist A. Q. Khan.

Furthermore, a North Korean representative had stated that the country possessed nuclear weapons – while not otherwise confirmed, this claim remains credible.

The Commission hopes that the six-party talks will induce North Korea to walk back from development of a nuclear weapon capability. The situation is dangerous for the region, and joint regional action and engagement will be important in defusing it. There are a number of elements which the Commission suggests might be relevant for a settlement, several of which are found in the 1992 Denuclearization Declaration and in the 1994 Agreed Framework, and some but not all of which are presently on the table:

- A starting point must be that guarantees have to be obtained from North Korea on the verified dismantlement of all nuclear weapons and nuclear installations together with items that have been linked to the weapon programme. This means not only rejoining and satisfying the NPT, but going beyond the requirements of the treaty to include shutting down any installations meant for the production of enriched uranium or the production of plutonium through the reprocessing of spent nuclear fuel. International inspection and monitoring would be required.

- As North Korea may possess chemical and biological weapons, its government should be required to eliminate all of these as well. Again, international inspection and monitoring would be required.

- The North Korean government – which sees South Korea as an economically strong and prosperous state with powerful allies, and which finds itself alienated from allies it used to have – will need assurances about its security.

- The commitments made in the 1992 Denuclearization Declaration between North and South Korea could be revived and be expanded to cover all WMD, effectively establishing a regional WMD-free zone, with effective inspection and monitoring. As envisaged in 1992 there would be no enrichment or reprocessing facilities on the peninsula. The supply of nuclear fuel and the disposal of spent nuclear fuel could be assured and guaranteed through a regional arrangement – at any rate for a prolonged period of time.

- Although a change of the economic and political system in North Korea is desirable, not least from the viewpoint of human rights, regime change should not be sought by the use of force from the outside or by subversion. Gradual change could be stimulated by trade and assistance, linking the country to its neighbours and the rest of the world.

- North Korea should be given the same kind of guarantees against outside attacks that were given in the Agreed Framework of 1994.
- Holding up the prospect of diplomatic relations would also signal an end to North Korea's isolation and the beginning of a reintegration with the world community. At the same time North Korea must abide by the requirements of respect for international law.

WMDC RECOMMENDATION

5 Negotiations with North Korea should aim at a verifiable agreement including, as a principal element, North Korea's manifesting its adherence to the Non-Proliferation Treaty and accepting the 1997 Additional Protocol, as well as a revival and legal confirmation of the commitments made in the 1992 Joint Declaration on the Denuclearization of the Korean Peninsula: notably, that neither North nor South Korea shall have nuclear weapons or nuclear reprocessing and uranium enrichment facilities. Fuel-cycle services should be assured through international arrangements. The agreement should also cover biological and chemical weapons, as well as the Comprehensive Nuclear-Test-Ban Treaty, thus making the Korean peninsula a zone free of weapons of mass destruction.

Iran's long-standing efforts to develop a capability to enrich uranium without reporting these activities to the IAEA have caused much concern and debate. While Iran firmly asserts that its efforts are intended only to give it an indigenous source of low-enriched uranium fuel for its planned nuclear power sector, many states suspect that the country would use this capability also to produce highly enriched uranium for nuclear weapons. They feel that this possibility must be closed sooner rather than later.

Findings by the IAEA confirm that Iran has repeatedly breached its nuclear safeguards agreement by not reporting the clandestine acquisition of uranium enrichment technology and materials from Pakistan through the A. Q. Khan supplier network.

France, Germany and the UK, acting with the support of the European Union, have pursued talks with Iran to seek an arrangement that would preserve Iran's right to the peaceful uses of nuclear energy without the operation of sensitive nuclear fuel-cycle facilities, specifically uranium enrichment and nuclear reprocessing plants. The EU, the US, Russia and China have maintained continuous and intensive contacts in this matter.

The Commission hopes that the high-level contacts between Iran, other governments and the IAEA, and negotiations in the Security Council will succeed in finding a generally acceptable solution. Valuable and detailed proposals for a way forward have been presented by influential independent organizations, including the International Crisis Group. The Commission views the following considerations as essential in the search for a solution:

- The pursuit of any enrichment and reprocessing activities by Iran would lead to sharply increased tension in the Middle East, which cannot be in the interest of Iran or any other state. It is desirable for Iran to fully suspend the efforts and defer the enrichment programme for a prolonged period of time.

- As it is very difficult to prove a negative, it is unlikely that the IAEA would ever be able to conclude with absolute certainty that Iran – or at least key elements within its governing system – have not had the intention to use an enrichment capability for weapon purposes. In any case, even if such intentions never existed, there could be a change of mind once Iran's enrichment technology was fully operational. Accordingly, the question of intention is not decisive.

- In the sensitive region of the Middle East, the long-term vision must include the establishment of a zone free of all WMD, which all states, including Iran and Israel, support. (In fact, the idea of a zone approach to WMD in the region dates back to 1974, when Egypt and Iran first proposed in the UN General Assembly the creation of a Middle East nuclear-weapon-free zone.) As the existence of enrichment or reprocessing activities raises fear, such activities should be suspended or deferred for a prolonged period of time, while any fuel-cycle services would be assured from the outside. The development of enrichment or reprocessing capabilities in Iran would raise new obstacles to the achievement of the common goal. While Israel, feeling under threat from Iran and others, is not likely to discard its nuclear-weapon capability except as a part of a peace settlement, it could help to reduce tension, as is now asked of Iran, by joining Iran and all other states in the region in a commitment to suspend and renounce any fuel-cycle activities for a prolonged period of time.

- A key premise of discussions with Iran and the resolutions passed by the Board of the IAEA has been that Iran, as all other parties to the NPT, has the right – in keeping with Articles II and IV of the treaty – to engage in peaceful nuclear energy production. While some have sought to suggest that this right does not extend to the right to domestically enrich uranium, but only to have a secure supply of fuel for power reactors, it would seem to be not only legally correct but also wise to recognize that there is a right for NPT states, acting in full conformity with Article II and IV of the treaty, to participate in all stages of fuel-cycle activity. Trying to reinterpret the NPT and assert a new division of the world into 'nuclear fuel-cycle-haves' and 'have-nots' would hardly get broad support.

- Nevertheless, a right to do something does not necessarily mean that this right must be exercised. Nothing prevents states in a sensitive region, like Iran and other states in the Middle East (or the two Korean states), from suspending or deferring any fuel-cycle activities, if their pursuit has negative consequences and suspension or deferment may bring economic or political advantages.

- It is important, accordingly, to present Iran with economic and political incentives to defer for a prolonged period of time any plans for fuel-cycle activities on its own soil, even as it reserves the right in principle to pursue such activities for peaceful purposes. The proposals presented by three European states rightly include such incentives.

- Iran, on completing the construction of two light-water nuclear power reactors, will need to be sure that it has a secure supply of low-enriched uranium reactor fuel. Reliable assurances of supply from the outside will be needed. This should be a manageable problem.

- Russia has offered to host an enrichment plant for Iran. The initiative would guarantee that only low-enriched uranium would be produced. It would also give valuable experience in the establishment and operation of a fuel-cycle installation in one country, designed to serve the needs of another country in the region. There is an obvious parallel with the case of Korea, where a renunciation of enrichment capability will require assurance of nuclear-fuel supplies from states outside, for instance Russia and China.

- Russia has agreed to take back all spent reactor fuel from Iran, thus freeing the country from the considerable problem of disposal and, at the same time, guaranteeing that no plutonium separation occurs in Iran.

- Questions relating to security might be significant. Iran might perceive itself as threatened by a US military presence in Iraq, the Gulf, Pakistan, Afghanistan and several other states in the region. As in the case of North Korea, guarantees against attacks from the outside may contribute to a solution. Promises of diplomatic relations rather than of isolation would undoubtedly also be seen as facilitating relaxed relations.

- While many powerful governments and influential mass media are critical of the political regime in Iran, it should be made clear in any agreement that regime change would not be sought by the use of force from the outside or by subversion. Any such change should be left to the people in Iran.

WMDC RECOMMENDATION

 6 Negotiations must be continued to induce Iran to suspend any sensitive fuel-cycle-related activities and ratify the 1997 Additional Protocol and resume full cooperation with the International Atomic Energy Agency in order to avoid an increase in tensions and to improve the outlook for the common aim of establishing a Middle East zone free of weapons of mass destruction. The international community and Iran should build mutual confidence through measures that should include: reliable assurance regarding the supply of fuel-cycle services; suspending or renouncing sensitive fuel-cycle activities for a prolonged period of time by all states in the Middle East; assurances against attacks and subversion aiming at regime change; and facilitation of international trade and investment.

Security assurances

A few days before the NPT was opened for signature in 1968, the UN Security Council adopted Resolution 255, consisting of positive security assurances that any non-nuclear-weapon state that is attacked with nuclear weapons or subject to the threat of such an attack would receive assistance. It was understandable that non-nuclear-weapon states would also seek additional legally binding assurances – known as negative security assurances – against attacks or threats of attack involving weapons that they have themselves legally renounced.

Support for this principle remains overwhelming and global in scope. Every year since 1978, including 2005, the UN General Assembly has adopted a resolution on negative nuclear security assurances. On the eve of the 1995 NPT Review and Extension Conference, all five nuclear-weapon states made statements concerning positive and negative security assurances to NPT non-nuclear-weapon states. France, Russia, the United Kingdom and the United States harmonized their negative security assurances, providing identical caveats and conditions relating to the inapplicability of such assurances in the case of a non-nuclear-weapon state engaging in aggression in association or alliance with a nuclear-weapon state. China gave an unconditional assurance and reiterated its no-first-use pledge. These statements were then referred to in Security Council Resolution 984 (1995), which superseded the 1968 assurances.

The Review and Extension Conference decided that 'further steps should be considered' to assure non-nuclear-weapon states against the use or threat of use of nuclear weapons, such as an internationally legally binding instrument. Also, the 2000 NPT Review Conference stated by consensus that legally binding security assurances would strengthen the nuclear non-proliferation regime.

The Commission agrees that the nuclear-weapon states parties to the NPT should provide *legally binding security assurances* to non-nuclear-weapon state parties to the NPT. The Commission notes that there is no objection in principle in the Conference on Disarmament (CD) to the negotiation of an agreement on negative security assurances. This issue has been on the CD's agenda for many years. The CD could consider moving forward with negotiations on a universal, multilateral treaty containing effective international arrangements to assure non-nuclear-weapon states against the use or threat of use of nuclear weapons.

WMDC RECOMMENDATION

7 The nuclear-weapon states parties to the Non-Proliferation Treaty should provide legally binding negative security assurances to non-nuclear-weapon states parties. The states not party to the Non-Proliferation Treaty that possess nuclear weapons should separately provide such assurances.

The fuel cycle: controlling the production of enriched uranium and plutonium

Most nuclear power reactors in the world use uranium enriched to some 4% as fuel; this is produced in a technically difficult process that may also allow enrichment to levels suitable for use in nuclear weapons – 85% or more. Technically, any enrichment plant can thus be used for the production of reactor fuel or bomb-grade material or both. It is a matter of political will. Currently enrichment plants exist in about a dozen states.

The spent fuel that comes out of the power reactors contains plutonium as well as unused uranium and various actinides. Currently most spent fuel – highly radioactive – is simply kept in intermediate storage. However, it may be sent for reprocessing in another technically difficult process, which recovers plutonium and uranium that can be used as new fuel in reactors. If this is done, the amount of waste remaining is greatly reduced and the amount of energy that is extracted from the original uranium is increased about one hundredfold. The plutonium obtained from spent reactor fuel can be used to make bombs but its isotopic composition is not ideal for the purpose. To obtain weapon-grade plutonium, nuclear-weapon states have reprocessed spent uranium fuel from special production reactors.

The production of highly enriched uranium and the separation of plutonium are regarded as raising the greatest difficulties for anyone wishing to make nuclear weapons. It is for this reason that the international safeguards system is geared to verify that there is no clandestine production or diversion of such material. It is also for this reason that many governments are concerned about Iran's development of an enrichment capability and North Korea's capability to separate plutonium and perhaps also enrich uranium. As described above, intense diplomatic efforts have been under way to induce North Korea to close its indigenous nuclear installations and Iran to defer for a prolonged period of time plans to enrich uranium.

There is another concern. It is widely expected that global reliance on nuclear power will increase in the next decades, as the price of fossil oil and gas goes up and the greenhouse gas-free nuclear energy becomes more attractive. If so, there will be a greater demand for uranium fuel, possibly leading to the construction of more enrichment plants. As reprocessing of spent fuel will allow a drastically better use of the energy content of the original uranium fuel, there may also be a demand for more reprocessing plants. The concern is that an increase in the number of enrichment and reprocessing plants and an increased flow of fissile material may increase the risk of misuse and diversion.

Fuel-cycle proposals

A growth of nuclear power will take time, and existing global capacity for enrichment and reprocessing is enough to meet the needs arising from a considerable expansion. Plans for additional plants are currently known to exist only in the United States. Nevertheless, interesting ideas have been presented describing how a steady supply of nuclear fuel could be produced and assured for a growing number of reactors without increasing the risk of misuse and diversion.

Under one proposal, a moratorium of several years should be accepted on the construction of new facilities for the enrichment of uranium or reprocessing. This would allow time to work out a scheme for the multinational control of all such facilities, wherever they are located. States complying with non-proliferation commitments should be able to turn to an international fuel bank and be assured that they could buy low-enriched nuclear fuel at market prices. The proposal would seek to make it attractive to turn to the bank for supply and, thereby, reduce any incentive for states to build their own enrichment or reprocessing facilities. An international framework, based upon agreed rules and in which both producers and consumers of enriched uranium fuel have a say about pricing and rights of purchase, might be sufficiently attractive to persuade consumers to renounce enrichment. However, many questions are left open. For instance, who would decide whether a country is fulfilling its non-proliferation commitments and thus is entitled to purchase enriched uranium?

Another scheme was advanced in 2006 by the United States and has been discussed with governments in London, Paris, Moscow, Beijing, New Delhi and Tokyo: The Global Nuclear Energy Partnership (GNEP). Under this scheme a small number of states would produce fuel for nuclear power reactors by enriching uranium. They would 'lease' the fuel to states – including developing countries, which are expected to increase their consumption of electricity – for use in power reactors and take back the spent fuel. They would thereafter reprocess the spent fuel in a new process, which would recover uranium and plutonium that would be mixed with some actinides to make it highly toxic and unsuitable as weapon material. It would be used as fuel in special reactors that would be built only in the fuel-producing states. The remaining volume of waste would be drastically smaller than the volume of spent fuel that was reprocessed.

'Fuel-cycle states' and 'user states'

A key goal of GNEP is to make the system attractive to states and thus reduce incentives to construct more enrichment or reprocessing plants. States would be free to rely on this system but would not be obliged to do so. If the 'fuel-cycle states' were to keep the nuclear waste that would result from the reprocessing, the scheme would have the great attraction of relieving the 'user states' of having to construct waste disposal facilities of their own. The intended benefit in the field of non-proliferation would be that the user states would have to commit themselves not to undertake any enrichment or reprocessing activities. Despite giving a growing number of states the opportunity to use nuclear power, the number of countries that would have facilities in which weapons-usable material could be produced would remain limited to a handful.

Although initial reactions to GNEP are reported to have been positive in the few states that have been consulted, it is evident that many questions – technical, economic and political – remain for governmental and public discussion. The scheme does tackle the proliferation and environmental concerns that would arise if enrichment plants, spent-fuel repositories and disposal sites were to be constructed widely in the world. There would be an economy of scale. The energy content of the uranium would be fully used.

On the other hand, it will not be known for many years whether the new type of reactors to burn the plutonium with some actinides is technically feasible. The political willingness of fuel-cycle states to accept the return of spent 'leased' nuclear fuel has not been tested. In the past, the former Soviet Union took back spent fuel from East European states as a non-proliferation measure, but generally states are averse to taking spent fuel or waste from other countries. Lastly, it is hard to predict whether it would be acceptable to add the inequality between fuel-cycle states and user states to the existing NPT inequality between nuclear-weapon states and non-nuclear-weapon states. Only the fuel-cycle states would be able to benefit from the new energy-efficient reactors. The deeper the cooperation between the fuel-cycle states, the more the group would look like a cartel of the powerful.

The schemes described, and others which will undoubtedly be advanced, deserve to be thoroughly discussed. There is time for such discussion. There is also a place where all states can take part. The IAEA has long served as a forum for considering proposals relating to the fuel cycle and for new types of nuclear power reactors. It is desirable that states continue to use the IAEA for these purposes, e.g. to discuss the ideas of fuel banks, regional arrangements for the production of fuel, and the management and disposal of spent fuel, as well as the possibility of proliferation-resistant fuel cycles.

Current problems

The above discussion considered long-term problems. However, there are also problems that cannot wait for long-term solutions but need to be tackled in the near future. North Korea and Iran present acute problems that were discussed above and that need early solutions. It is evident, however, that all countries possessing an enrichment or reprocessing capability are technically able – just like the states that have nuclear weapons – to make nuclear material that can be used in weapons. This is true of Brazil and Japan. In Japan, a large plant for the reprocessing of spent nuclear fuel will be opened in 2006 and will further increase an already large stockpile of plutonium. To some this is a concern. However, a decision to proceed to use available plutonium for weapons is a matter of political will. Hardly any plant in the world has prepared more thoroughly for the operation of IAEA safeguards than the Japanese reprocessing plant at Aomori.

Even today the risks of diversion of fissile material for weapon use could be somewhat reduced if highly enriched uranium production were phased out and plutonium separation were reduced. These possibilities should be explored.

Highly enriched uranium is used mainly in the nuclear propulsion of ships and in specific types of research reactors. In both cases, technological efforts are already under way in several countries to develop alternative fuels that cannot be directly used in making nuclear explosives. While a phasing out of all production of highly enriched uranium will not eliminate the possible use of enrichment plants for the production of highly enriched weapons-grade uranium, it would reduce the volume of such uranium.

Spent nuclear reactor fuel is reprocessed into plutonium on a large scale in a few countries. Originally, the idea was to utilize the considerable energy value of the plutonium by using the plutonium as fuel in breeder reactors. However, although reprocessing reduces the amount of waste that has to be disposed of, the economic reasons for this activity largely disappeared, because the cost of reprocessing was relatively high and the price of new uranium remained low. Today some of this plutonium is stored and some is mixed with uranium and used as 'mixed oxide fuel' in power reactors. Only relatively small amounts of plutonium are actually needed for the original purpose, namely, to serve as fuel in a small number of breeder reactors.

WMDC RECOMMENDATION

8 States should make active use of the IAEA as a forum for exploring various ways to reduce proliferation risks connected with the nuclear fuel cycle, such as proposals for an international fuel bank; internationally safeguarded regional centres offering fuel-cycle services, including spent-fuel repositories; and the creation of a fuel-cycle system built on the concept that a few 'fuel-cycle states' will lease nuclear fuel to states that forgo enrichment and reprocessing activities.

WMDC RECOMMENDATION

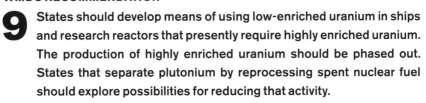

9 States should develop means of using low-enriched uranium in ships and research reactors that presently require highly enriched uranium. The production of highly enriched uranium should be phased out. States that separate plutonium by reprocessing spent nuclear fuel should explore possibilities for reducing that activity.

Fissile material clean-out

The G8 Global Partnership and other programmes – including the Cooperative Threat Reduction programme, the US Global Threat Reduction Initiative (GTRI), the Nuclear Threat Initiative, as well as initiatives by the European Union and other organizations – all contain efforts to reduce specific threats arising from WMD technology and materials.

BOX 9

EXAMPLES OF GLOBAL CLEAN-OUT ACTIVITIES

- Returning exported nuclear material to suppliers for secure disposal or elimination.
- Converting research reactors from highly enriched to low-enriched uranium fuel.
- Enhancing the security of highly enriched uranium used to produce radio-isotopes.
- Consolidating fissile material at centralized, highly secure locations.
- Ending the stockpiling of highly enriched uranium at fuel fabrication plants.

The United States and Russia, the states with the most research reactors fuelled by highly enriched uranium and that have exported most such reactors, have agreed at high-level summit meetings to deepen their cooperation in this global clean-out. The US Congress, having originated the Cooperative Threat Reduction programme in the Nunn-Lugar legislation, has long given firm support to many of these initiatives.

As suggested by the examples cited in Box 9, the global clean-out involves activities that extend beyond the goal of converting research reactors to use lower enriched fuel. Later in this chapter, the Commission discusses other related initiatives concerning physical protection, the disposal of fissile material recovered from warheads, and the proposal for a fissile material cut-off treaty.

WMDC RECOMMENDATION

10 All states should support the international initiatives taken to advance the global clean-out of fissile material. Such support should encompass the conversion of research reactors from highly enriched to low-enriched uranium fuel, storing fissile material at centralized and secure locations, and returning exported nuclear materials to suppliers for secure disposal or elimination.

Regional issues and arrangements

Nuclear-weapon-free zones

In the late 1940s and 1950s, the failure to outlaw nuclear weapons led some governments to look for intermediate steps towards that goal. One such initiative was to ban the stationing, testing, use or development of nuclear weapons in certain geographic areas – nuclear-weapon-free zones. Early efforts focused on unpopulated areas or environments, resulting in treaties covering Antarctica, the seabed and outer space.

The Tlatelolco Treaty, signed in 1967, broke new ground by seeking to include within the designated zone the entire populated region of Latin America and the Caribbean. The Treaties of Rarotonga (1986), Pelindaba (1996) and Bangkok (1997) created nuclear-weapon-free zones in the South Pacific, Africa, and Southeast Asia. Also, five former Soviet republics have provisionally agreed upon the text of a treaty to establish a nuclear-weapon-free zone in Central Asia. The concept of nuclear-weapon-free zones has emerged as a success story.

Nuclear-weapon-free zones serve some important functions. They fill the gap in the NPT that allowed the foreign deployment of nuclear weapons on the territory of non-nuclear-weapon states – no such weapons may be stationed in the zones. They complement and reinforce the basic non-proliferation commitments of the NPT. Through protocols to the treaties creating such zones, the nuclear-weapon states can provide legally binding negative security assurances to members of such regimes. They also contribute to the strengthening of comprehensive ('full-scope') IAEA safeguards, by requiring the domestic application and/or requirement of such safeguards for exports leaving the region. Furthermore, they help to strengthen the global norm against nuclear testing, pending entry into force of the CTBT.

These regimes, however, face many challenges. For instance, the Pelindaba Treaty, although almost a decade old, has still not entered into force. Of all the protocols to the nuclear-weapon-free zone treaties, only the relevant protocol to the Tlatelolco Treaty has been ratified by all five nuclear-weapon states. None of the nuclear-weapon states has ratified the protocol to the Bangkok Treaty, although China has said that it may agree to it independently of the other nuclear-weapon states.

In addition, many states in the zones have failed to conclude their required full-scope safeguards agreements with the IAEA. And while all the treaties creating such zones are of indefinite duration, they all contain withdrawal clauses. This opens questions about the reversibility of the commitments made.

WMDC RECOMMENDATION

11 All Non-Proliferation Treaty nuclear-weapon states that have not yet done so should ratify the protocols of the treaties creating regional nuclear-weapon-free zones. All states in such zones should conclude their comprehensive safeguards agreements with the IAEA and agree to ratify and implement the Additional Protocol.

The Middle East

The issue of Iran's enrichment of uranium is discussed above under the heading of the Non-Proliferation Treaty. Other nuclear issues in the Middle East region are related to Israel, which is not a party to the NPT and has significant nuclear-weapon capabilities; operational, unsafeguarded, nuclear activities; and a variety of nuclear-capable delivery systems. As long as the world community continues to postpone these issues, which are evidently linked to the question of peace and security in the region, they will add to the risk of the further proliferation of nuclear weapons and other WMD in the Middle East.

Israel's right to security must be guaranteed, as must the right to security of all other states in the Middle East. In 1995, NPT states parties addressed one vital dimension of this challenge by including the Middle East Resolution in the package deal that led to the indefinite extension of the treaty. This resolution endorsed the goals of the peace process and called for the establishment of 'an effectively verifiable Middle East zone free of weapons of mass destruction, nuclear, chemical and biological, and their delivery systems, and to refrain from taking any measures that preclude the achievement of this objective.' So far, however, the efforts to establish such a zone – a goal that all countries in the region, including Iran and Israel, have long supported – have not led to concrete negotiations.

Many initiatives have been proposed in recent years to break this impasse, including a proposal for the establishment of a WMD-free zone in the Gulf as a stepping stone to a wider regional zone. There are specific steps that may advance the security interests of all states in the region, while promoting the aim of a WMD-free zone in the Middle East. One would be for Israel, Egypt and Iran to proceed from signature to ratification of the CTBT, as all other states in the region have done. Another would address the problem of fissile materials. States in the region, including Israel, could defer or renounce for a prolonged period of time any enrichment or reprocessing activities on their territories. These and other confidence-building measures would facilitate the eventual establishment of a regional WMD-free zone, while also advancing the broader objectives of the peace process.

Israel, Egypt and Iran have only signed the CTBT. They should ratify the treaty, as the other states in the Middle East have done. A confidence-building measure that would be a step in a process that could eventually lead to a WMD-free zone would, as suggested above, be verified commitments by all states in the region, including Israel, to defer or renounce for a prolonged period of time any enrichment or reprocessing activities on their territories.

WMDC RECOMMENDATION

12 All states should support continued efforts to establish a zone free of weapons of mass destruction in the Middle East as a part of the overall peace process. Steps can be taken even now. As a confidence-building measure, all states in the region, including Iran and Israel, should for a prolonged period of time commit themselves to a verified arrangement not to have any enrichment, reprocessing or other sensitive fuel-cycle activities on their territories. Such a commitment should be coupled with reliable assurances about fuel-cycle services required for peaceful nuclear activities. Egypt, Iran and Israel should join the other states in the Middle East in ratifying the CTBT.

South Asia

Neither India nor Pakistan is a party to the NPT, and they are not expected to renounce their nuclear-weapon capability and form a zone free of WMD. Both countries have tested nuclear weapons, both are involved in producing more of them and improving them, both have announced military doctrines based on deterrence, and both are also developing different types of long-range missiles to deliver such weapons.

This does not mean that nothing can be done – or is being done – by India and Pakistan and others to reduce the risks linked to the tension between the two countries and to the WMD they possess. Both countries maintain unilateral nuclear-testing moratoria. They should both ratify the CTBT. Both support the goal of concluding an international fissile material treaty, although they differ on whether it should cover stocks of such material. They should join other states possessing nuclear weapons in declaring a moratorium on the production of further fissile material for weapons, pending the conclusion of an FMCT. The two countries have in recent years made some progress in mutual confidence building. They have concluded some high-level agreements to renounce attacks on nuclear facilities, to implement other measures to improve the transparency of military activities (including missile tests) and to reduce the risk of nuclear attacks. They should continue on this path.

India and the United States have been discussing renewed cooperation in the peaceful uses of nuclear energy and in March 2006 President Bush and Prime Minister Singh agreed on future cooperation between India and the US in the nuclear field.

While the agreement has many aspects, including some that are linked to global energy challenges, it has raised controversy from the viewpoint of non-proliferation. It envisages a number of Indian civilian nuclear installations to be placed under IAEA safeguards, but these installations do not include the Indian breeder reactor, nor stocks of spent fuel from reactors that remain unsafeguarded. Furthermore, the criticism has been voiced that, by allowing the import of nuclear reactor fuel or material for fuel, the agreement could facilitate India's production of weapons-usable fissile material and would be in questionable conformity with the NPT.

Article IV of the treaty provides that the fullest possible exchange should take place between the parties regarding the peaceful uses of nuclear energy. Neither this nor any other article of the treaty prohibits a party from agreeing on exchanges with states that are not parties to the treaty, provided that such exchanges do not 'assist' such states in the production of weapons (Article II). The Guidelines of the Nuclear Suppliers Group, in contrast, stipulate that the members should not export any nuclear equipment or material to states that do not have IAEA safeguards on all their present and future nuclear activities – in practice non-NPT parties, like India.

While it is thus clear that the draft US-India agreement would require modifications in the Guidelines of the NSG, its compatibility with the NPT is a matter of judgement. A party to the NPT is required to make only such agreements on nuclear cooperation that are consistent with the objective and purpose of the treaty. Concerns raised about the agreement in this regard would disappear if it were supplemented by action that demonstrated both parties' support for non-proliferation and disarmament.

The most reassuring such action would be an Indian and a US commitment to promote and participate without delay in a verifiable international treaty stopping all production of fissile material for weapons. Their adherence to such a treaty would dispel any fear that the agreement could facilitate an increased production of nuclear weapons in India and risk fuelling an arms race in Asia. Similarly, a commitment by the US and India to ratify the Comprehensive Nuclear-Test-Ban Treaty would send a signal that the intentions of the two states are to promote peaceful, not military, uses of nuclear energy.

WMDC RECOMMENDATION

13 India and Pakistan should both ratify the CTBT and join those other states with nuclear weapons that have declared a moratorium on the production of fissile material for weapons, pending the con-clusion of a treaty. They should continue to seek bilateral détente and build confidence through political, economic and military measures, reducing the risk of armed conflict, and increasing transparency in the nuclear and missile activities of both countries. Eventually, both states should become members of the Nuclear Suppliers Group and the Missile Technology Control Regime, as well as parties to International Atomic Energy Agency safeguards agreements under the terms of the 1997 Additional Protocol.

PREVENTING NUCLEAR TERRORISM

How could terrorists acquire nuclear weapons?

Nobody can make a nuclear weapon without two basic commodities – fissile material and the technical knowledge to design and manufacture such a device. It is generally understood that producing the fissile material on a sufficient scale is the more difficult task and that designing a weapon, while by no means easy, is the less difficult one. The basic information needed to design a crude nuclear explosive device is publicly available.

To produce the plutonium or highly enriched uranium needed to make nuclear weapons is difficult and expensive. It requires the kind of infra-structure that is likely to be available only to states. There is a risk, however, that security weaknesses could allow terrorists to steal enough material, or even an actual device. The most crucial step in preventing nuclear terrorism is, therefore, to keep terrorists from acquiring access to such materials or devices, a step that requires strict implementation of physical protection measures and security routines wherever such materials exist.

Important practical measures can be put in place to limit the available sources, increase physical security, increase safety where transportation is deemed unavoidable, and block terrorist access through better intelligence and security. Export controls and customs enforcement activities also serve vitally important roles in reducing the risk of nuclear terrorism.

Most experts believe that any would-be nuclear terrorist would probably prefer highly enriched uranium as a fissile material, because the 'gun-assembly' design, which uses this material, is simpler than the designs relying on plutonium. Yet one cannot exclude the possibility of a terrorist plutonium bomb – given that smaller amounts of such material are needed for it and that knowledge about implosion designs is more widely distributed today than in the days of the first plutonium bomb.

Given these risks, both highly enriched uranium and plutonium merit security controls as strict as those prescribed for nuclear weapons, a control that the US National Academy of Sciences has described as the stored-weapon standard.

Dirty bombs

Nuclear terrorists may seek to make not only nuclear explosive devices, but also radiological weapons, or dirty bombs. They might also seek to disperse radio-activity by attacks on nuclear facilities that produce, store or use hazardous radioactive materials, including spent nuclear fuel or nuclear materials in transit.

There are many ways in which terrorists could disperse hazardous nuclear material to contaminate specific target areas or create mass panic. Using radioactive substances, stolen for instance from research labs or hospitals, they could simply detonate a small conventional explosive surrounded by such material, or release it directly as a gas or powder. Although radioactive dispersal is not likely to produce great numbers of immediate fatalities, as does a nuclear weapon, dirty bombs are much easier to make than fission weapons and can cause considerable terror and disruption, especially if detonated in the heart of major cities.

A convention on nuclear terrorism

In 2005 the UN General Assembly adopted the International Convention for the Suppression of Acts of Nuclear Terrorism. As of April 2006, it has 102 signatories. The Convention requires the domestic criminalization of acts of nuclear terrorism and commits its parties to international cooperation in the prevention, investigation and prosecution of acts of nuclear terrorism. While offering no panacea, this convention is a significant and welcome achievement. States should proceed to early ratification and implementation.

Physical protection measures

The physical protection of fissile material and the physical security of nuclear weapons refer to controls designed to prevent sabotage, attacks, thefts and other such criminal acts. By ensuring early detection, prevention and recovery of missing materials, physical security controls also seek to discourage such illicit uses. States with nuclear weapons have their own command-and-control procedures to maintain the physical security of such weapons.

While all states have a common interest in physical protection to prevent nuclear terrorism, governments have long preferred to manage such threats primarily through domestic laws and policies. Recent multilateral efforts to improve these standards are summarized in Box 10.

Physical protection involves far more than just guards, gates and fences at particular facilities. It also requires reliable personnel to design and implement such controls, employing people who have both technical competence and professionalism. This entails extensive background checks before recruitment and thorough training after.

BOX 10

RECENT INTERNATIONAL EFFORTS TO STRENGTHEN PHYSICAL PROTECTION

- In 2001, the IAEA secretariat prepared a set of Physical Protection Objectives and Fundamental Principles, later endorsed by the IAEA Board of Governors. The IAEA also assists states through its International Physical Protection Advisory Service, and has developed a plan of action against nuclear terrorism supported by an extra-budgetary Nuclear Security (Multi-Donor) Fund.
- In June 2002, the G8 Global Partnership against the Spread of Weapons and Materials of Mass Destruction stressed the need for 'appropriate effective physical protection'.
- In 2003, the IAEA approved a revised Code of Conduct on the Safety and Security of Radioactive Sources. The Agency has issued several reports and adopted several resolutions on Measures to Protect Against Nuclear Terrorism.
- In 2004, the Security Council adopted Resolution 1540, which requires all states to 'develop and maintain appropriate effective physical protection measures'.
- As of 2005, and pursuant to the US Nunn-Lugar (1991) and Nunn-Lugar-Domenici laws (1996), the US has invested over $5 billion in WMD disarmament-related activities in Russia, a quarter of which has been spent on improving nuclear security.

While states have the legal responsibility for maintaining physical security of nuclear materials within their borders, the IAEA has published some common standards (contained in Information Circular 225) for the transportation of such materials, in accordance with the multilateral Convention on the Physical Protection of Nuclear Material, which has 116 states parties as of March 2006. These controls serve as a basic model for state regulatory authorities to follow in implementing their own controls.

Growing challenges and responses

Concerns over the physical security of nuclear weapons and fissile material have grown due to a number of developments. These include reports of the illicit trafficking in radioactive materials (including small amounts of fissile material); chronic security problems at nuclear facilities in Russia and other former Soviet republics; claims that terrorist groups are seeking to acquire radioactive or fissile material for nuclear weapons or so-called dirty bombs and worries, in the post-9/11 environment, of the possibility of terrorist attacks at civilian nuclear facilities.

Although states apply and implement their own standards, the chain of physical security is only as strong as its weakest link. The theft of fissile material somewhere can jeopardize security everywhere. Such concerns have inspired many international initiatives in this area, as summarized in Box 10.

Many obstacles hinder further progress in strengthening physical security controls. International cooperation is inhibited by governmental concerns over the erosion of sovereignty, legal liability, budgetary constraints, etc. Such obstacles also hinder the development of stronger multilateral standards or expanded roles for international institutions. The lack of serious consequences for non-compliance with existing standards further erodes both the effectiveness and credibility of those standards.

As a practical matter, many improvements in international physical security standards have had to await the stimulus provided by shocking events, as seen in the interest in physical security shown by many states after 9/11.

WMDC RECOMMENDATION

14   States must prevent terrorists from gaining access to nuclear weapons or fissile material. To achieve this, they must maintain fully effective accounting and control of all stocks of fissile and radio-active material and other radiological sources on their territories. They should ensure that there is personal legal responsibility for any acts of nuclear terrorism or activities in support of such terrorism. They must expand their cooperation through *inter alia* the sharing of information, including intelligence on illicit nuclear commerce. They should also promote universal adherence to the International Convention for the Suppression of Acts of Nuclear Terrorism and to the Convention on the Physical Protection of Nuclear Material and implementation of UN Security Council Resolution 1540.

REDUCING THE THREAT AND THE NUMBERS OF EXISTING NUCLEAR WEAPONS

Many of the world's estimated 27,000 nuclear weapons remain on hair-trigger alert, which raises the risks of accidents, misunderstandings and even deliberate use. Moreover, the Commission has noted with concern the statements made by senior officials of a few states possessing nuclear weapons in which they suggest – some more explicitly than others – that their countries might one day use nuclear weapons in retaliation for terrorist attacks, aggression involving the use of other WMD, or even certain attacks involving conventional weapons. As recently as January 2006, French President Jacques Chirac warned that:

'*The leaders of States who would use terrorist means against us, as well as those who would consider using, in one way or another, weapons of mass destruction, must understand that they would lay themselves open to a firm and adapted response on our part. And this response could be a conventional one. It could also be of a different kind.*'

This and statements by other leaders in effect brandishing nuclear weapons, including in circumstances where there is no obvious military rationale (given, *inter alia*, the effectiveness of contemporary conventional weapons, and the implausibility of terrorist groups being deterred by threats of nuclear retaliation) point to an urgent need to reduce the role of nuclear weapons in the security policies of states and to drastically and progressively reduce the number of such weapons. The Commission identifies several initiatives to help pursue these aims, relating to doctrines, deployments and the development of weapons.

The need to re-examine and revise nuclear doctrines

Each state that has acquired nuclear weapons has also devised plans and principles – a military doctrine – on how its nuclear forces are to be configured and employed. These doctrines influence the choices of weapons to develop and produce, the capabilities needed to deliver them and the various constraints on their use. Such doctrines have an impact also on the planning and postures of other countries that are trying to protect their own security interests.

Despite improvements in their bilateral relations, the five nuclear-weapon states parties to the NPT continue to watch each other warily, while maintaining and modernizing their strategic nuclear capabilities. They are even espousing new nuclear doctrines that emphasize first-use, for instance to deter or retaliate against the use of other WMD, as noted above.

There has long been a close relationship between Soviet (later Russian) and NATO nuclear doctrines. China is watching to see if the United States intends and succeeds to follow through on its stated intention to make missile defence a more prominent part of its strategic doctrine. Israel chooses not to declare whether or not it possesses nuclear weapons – and this doctrine of nuclear ambiguity affects the security thinking of its neighbours, as would an open declaration of possession of nuclear weapons.

Whenever a nuclear-weapon state declares that all options are on the table, that it reserves the option of using nuclear weapons against a non-nuclear-weapon state, or that nuclear weapons are essential or vital for its security, other states take note and act accordingly.

At the heart of all these doctrines is the concept of deterrence.

Nuclear deterrence

Proponents of nuclear deterrence hold that the most reliable means for a country to prevent a nuclear attack is to dissuade a possible attacker by showing that it will survive such an attack and retain the capability and will to launch a devastating nuclear counter-strike. This situation, a dramatic manifestation of the notion of balance of terror that prevailed between the United States and the Soviet Union during the last three decades of the Cold War, came to be called mutual assured destruction (MAD).

Many observers believe that nuclear deterrence prevented a major war between the United States and the Soviet Union during the years of Cold War confrontation and conflicts. Others argue that the absence of such a war was due to many other factors, including a lack of reasons for going to war and sheer luck. But even if mutual deterrence stabilized the strategic relationship between the two superpowers during the Cold War, the relevance of nuclear deterrence has become increasingly questioned in the Post-Cold War period. It is not likely to prevent further proliferation of nuclear weapons, nor their actual use by governments acting recklessly or by terrorists.

Nevertheless, despite the fundamental changes in the political map of the world and despite the historic Joint Declaration by Presidents Bush and Putin of 13 November 2001 that 'neither country regards the other as an enemy or threat', nuclear deterrence doctrines remain on the books.

But even though governments frequently invoke deterrence as a rationale for retaining nuclear weapons, its relevance has sharply diminished if not completely vanished. It originated in the effort to avert the danger of war in a bipolar nuclear world that no longer exists. Invoking it in a very changed world tends to keep mistrust alive and inhibit the closer international cooperation necessary to address common problems, including the threats of nuclear proliferation and catastrophic terrorism.

First-use, pre-emption and prevention

While in the past the essence of nuclear deterrence was to demonstrate an effective capability for a retaliatory strike to deter a nuclear or large-scale conventional attack against one's own nation or its allies, now a number of nuclear-weapon states (France, Russia, the United Kingdom and the United States) go beyond this position and give nuclear weapons a more varied role. They now say that they are prepared for the first-use of nuclear weapons in regional and local wars and in various selective ways (e.g. to destroy deeply buried underground hardened sites). Some states with nuclear weapons, including India, Russia, the United Kingdom, France and the United States, also maintain the option of the first use of nuclear weapons in retaliation for an attack involving other types of WMD. Of the NPT nuclear-weapon states, only China has formally renounced the first use of nuclear weapons.

The UN Charter is generally interpreted as allowing the use of armed force in self-defence by a state that is facing an armed attack or to pre-empt an imminent armed attack. In 2002, however, the United States went beyond this concept of pre-emption and announced that it would reserve the right to use force, including nuclear weapons, to prevent an attack possibly involving

WMD, even if the time, place and scale of such WMD attack were uncertain and not imminent.

The Commission finds that military doctrines providing for the first or preventive use of nuclear weapons, or for use in retaliation for attacks with weapons other than nuclear, all tend to widen the licence in the doctrine of nuclear deterrence for actual nuclear war-fighting. They all risk lowering the threshold for the use of nuclear weapons. They expand the range of scenarios for the military use of such weapons and are an incentive to develop new nuclear weapons, all in direct contradiction of commitments made to strive for nuclear disarmament and all to the detriment of international security.

In Europe, the first-use nuclear doctrines of Russia and NATO nuclear-weapon states serve no credible military purpose in a Post-Cold War world. They glaringly contradict the efforts of these countries to work together for economic and cultural integration, to coordinate sensitive matters such as the interoperability of peacekeeping forces, and to cooperate in several WMD-related fields.

Readiness for use

Nuclear doctrines also dictate how nuclear weapons will be employed and their readiness for use. Thousands of US and Russian strategic nuclear warheads are deployed in a so-called *triad* consisting of submarine-launched missiles, ground-based intercontinental ballistic missiles, and long-range aircraft. Continuing a triad policy leads to redundancy and may fuel the nuclear arms race. Many such weapons remain on hair-trigger alert and are still assigned for retaliatory use on short notice – even before the warheads of one side reach the other's territory. Since the flight time of US and Russian land-based missiles is between 25 and 30 minutes – significantly less for sea-based missiles – such nuclear postures risk causing nuclear exchanges by accident, technical malfunction or strategic miscalculation.

In 1991, then-President George H.W. Bush took the first steps in the early Post-Cold War era to reducing the risks linked to a high operational readiness of nuclear weapons. He ordered a reduction of the level of alert, after which most of the US nuclear weapons were unloaded from strategic bombers and put into storage. In 1998, Britain announced that the notice to fire Trident missiles would require days rather than hours. Finally in 2000, the five nuclear powers announced that their weapons were no longer permanently targeted on specific sites in such countries.

While these decisions reduce the risks of accidents, they can also be reversed at any given time. Missiles deployed in silos can be re-targeted and fired in minutes.

BOX 11

THE TERMINOLOGY OF READINESS

Launch-on-warning is a nuclear posture intended to ensure quick responses in the event of a missile attack. It requires early-warning and command-and-control systems that use satellites to detect a missile launch from any location on the globe. These systems then reconfirm the launch with long-range radars and provide assessments to the political leadership, which may deliver a launch authorization to ICBM command posts and strategic submarines at sea. Given the short flight times of such missiles, the launch-on-warning posture leaves the political leadership only minutes for taking the most dramatic decision imaginable – authorizing a large-scale nuclear war.

Hair-trigger alert applies to missile forces and their early-warning and command-and-control systems. It is the readiness needed for a launch-on-warning posture.

Depending on the weapon system and level of desired alert status, there are several additional approaches to reducing the danger of accidental nuclear war. The most urgent task is to eliminate the launch-on-warning posture (see Box 11), a goal that may require some innovative verification measures. If agreed bilaterally, these could include the participation of inspectors from both countries in military exercises of their strategic forces or even a permanent presence of liaison officers at their strategic command posts.

A more far-reaching, verifiable, less reversible, and hence desirable, measure would be to make it technically impossible to launch strategic weapons on short notice, both for a surprise first strike and on warning of such an attack. Such measures would include removing warheads from delivery vehicles and putting them in storage, and removing missile nose cones and other such actions.

It is sometimes said that military leaders dislike nuclear weapons, because while requiring considerable resources they remain 'theoretical' weapons that cannot be relied upon in ordinary military planning. It is high time that this sentiment be allowed to migrate into military doctrine. Regrettably and paradoxically, current doctrines seem to allow a wider use of nuclear weapons than those that applied during the Cold War.

WMDC RECOMMENDATION

15

All states possessing nuclear weapons should declare a categorical policy of no-first-use of such weapons. They should specify that this covers both pre-emptive and preventive action, as well as retaliation for attacks involving chemical, biological or conventional weapons.

WMDC RECOMMENDATION

16

All states possessing nuclear weapons should review their military plans and define what is needed to maintain credible non-nuclear security policies. States deploying their nuclear forces in triads, consisting of submarine-launched missiles, ground-based intercontinental ballistic missiles and long-range bombers, should abandon this practice in order to reduce nuclear-weapon redundancy and avoid fuelling nuclear arms races.

WMDC RECOMMENDATION

17

Russia and the United States should agree on reciprocal steps to take their nuclear weapons off hair-trigger alert and should create a joint commission to facilitate this goal. They should undertake to eliminate the launch-on-warning option from their nuclear war plans, while implementing a controlled parallel decrease in operational readiness of a large part of their strategic forces, through:

- reducing the number of strategic submarines at sea and lowering their technical readiness to launch while in port;
- storing nuclear bombs and air-launched cruise missiles separately from relevant air fields;
- storing separately nose cones and/or warheads of most intercontinental ballistic missiles or taking other technical measures to reduce their readiness.

Deployment of nuclear weapons

The Commission believes that, more than a decade after the end of the Cold War, deeper cuts in strategic nuclear weapons are overdue, and new restraints are equally overdue on non-strategic nuclear weapons.

Bilateral reductions by Russia and the United States

The 1991 START I Treaty was followed in 1993 by START II, which provided for a two-phased process of reducing US and Russian deployed strategic nuclear warheads down to 3,000–3,500 for each state. The Joint Statement issued in 1997 after the Clinton-Yeltsin summit at Helsinki contained a framework agreement to pursue these specific objectives in START III, marking the high point in the bilateral Russian–US efforts to achieve an effective reduction in warhead numbers. However, due to the unilateral termination of the ABM Treaty caused by the US wish to pursue a strategic missile defence programme, START II never entered into force and negotiations on START III were never initiated.

The START treaties only limit the numbers of deployed strategic warheads and their related delivery vehicles. They also do not require the physical destruction of any nuclear warheads.

When such weapons have actually been destroyed, this has occurred more in order to reduce obvious redundancies or to replace aging weapons than to advance any positive disarmament objective.

This tradition continued in the bilateral Strategic Offensive Reductions Treaty (SORT) of 2002, in which Russia and the United States agreed to reduce the deployment of strategic nuclear weapons down to levels of 1,700–2,200 weapons per country by 2012. While continuing the positive downward trend in deployments, this treaty does not involve any destruction of warheads, as they will simply be put into storage, nor any counting rules or new verification measures. Under SORT, deployments change but the weapons remain.

WMDC RECOMMENDATION

18 Russia and the United States should commence negotiations on a new strategic arms reduction treaty aimed at reducing their deployments of strategic forces allowed under the Strategic Offensive Reductions Treaty by at least half. It should include a legally binding commitment to irreversibly dismantle the weapons withdrawn under the Strategic Offensive Reductions Treaty. The new treaty should also include transparent counting rules, schedules and procedures for dismantling the weapons, and reciprocal measures for verification.

WMDC RECOMMENDATION

19   Russia and the United States, followed by other states possessing nuclear weapons, should publish their aggregate holdings of nuclear weapons on active and reserve status as a baseline for future disarmament efforts. They should also agree to include specific provisions in future disarmament agreements relating to transparency, irreversibility, verification and the physical destruction of nuclear warheads.

Initiatives involving all states possessing nuclear weapons

It is often forgotten that the NPT nuclear disarmament commitment applies to all states parties. The 'package deal' that enabled the indefinite extension of the treaty in 1995 included a call for this goal to be 'fulfilled with determination' and urged the nuclear-weapon states to make systematic and progressive efforts to reduce nuclear weapons globally.

This was in 1995. It is easy to see that the nuclear-weapon states parties to the NPT have largely failed to implement this commitment and failed to 'pursue negotiations in good faith' on nuclear disarmament as required of them under the NPT. Indeed, all states that have nuclear weapons are still seeking to modernize their nuclear capabilities.

There is an urgent need for a change of attitude and for progress in this area. Whether or not parties to the NPT, states that have acquired nuclear weapons must decide without further delay how they can contribute to the nuclear disarmament process. The United States and Russia have huge nuclear arsenals that no longer serve the original purpose of mutual deterrence. They have also not engaged in any serious bilateral disarmament talks since concluding SORT in 2002. Progress in implementing the deep reductions proposed above would encourage some downward movement in the size of nuclear arsenals in other states. Individually or jointly, all state possessing such weapons must participate in this global effort. Having unilaterally decided long ago to enter the nuclear club, all nuclear-weapon states must now recognize that it is their duty to exit.

France and the UK will have to decide whether it will be meaningful to retain costly nuclear arsenals that were developed for an enemy that no longer exists, in order to meet hypothetical threats against which such weapons are of questionable value. Both countries are now at a crossroads: going down one road would show their conviction that nuclear weapons are not necessary for their security, while the other would demonstrate to all other states a belief that these weapons continue to be indispensable. In addition, by pursuing their security interests without nuclear weapons, they would avoid the need for costly investments in dangerous new nuclear capabilities or replacements for existing weapons.

China must also contribute to the disarmament effort. The policies it pursues have impacts at both the global and the regional level. China should be more transparent about its policies and its nuclear capability. By ratifying the CTBT, China would help to build pressure for more ratifications and entry into force. China should also unilaterally declare that, pending an FMCT, it will refrain from producing fissile material for weapon purposes.

Israel should ratify the CTBT. Israel should unilaterally close its sensitive fuel-cycle installations and, unilaterally or in parallel with other countries in the Middle East, renounce any fuel-cycle-related activities for a prolonged period of time. India and Pakistan should sign and ratify the CTBT and declare a moratorium on the production of fissile material for weapons purposes pending an FMCT.

WMDC RECOMMENDATION

20 All states possessing nuclear weapons must address the issue of their continued possession of such weapons. All nuclear-weapon states parties to the Non-Proliferation Treaty must take steps towards nuclear disarmament, as required by the treaty and the commitments made in connection with the treaty's indefinite extension. Russia and the United States should take the lead. Other states possessing nuclear weapons should join the process, individually or in coordinated action. While Israel, India and Pakistan are not parties to the Non-Proliferation Treaty, they, too, have a duty to contribute to the nuclear disarmament process.

New limits on deployments of non-strategic nuclear weapons

The end of the Cold War led to major reductions in the deployments of tactical, or non-strategic, nuclear weapons (see Box 12). The Presidential Nuclear Initiatives of 1991 between Presidents Bush and Gorbachev, confirmed by President Yeltsin in 1992, were in the form of unilateral undertakings to eliminate or dramatically reduce nuclear warheads deployed on short-range ballistic missiles, nuclear artillery shells and nuclear mines, as well as to remove or reduce those weapons deployed on surface warships, such as nuclear depth charges.

NON-STRATEGIC NUCLEAR WEAPONS – some definitions

Other terms: 'tactical nuclear weapons', 'sub-strategic nuclear weapons'

In general, 'non-strategic' refers to weapons with a tactical role on the battle-field and that are not intended for use against an enemy's nuclear missiles or population centres. Yet the distinction has become difficult if not impossible to sustain, particularly in regional settings. Such weapons include short-range missiles, artillery shells and nuclear mines.

Yield: This may vary from low to very high. As an example, the yield of the B61 gravity bomb may be set from 0.3 kilotons to 170 kilotons (i.e., 14 times the yield of the Hiroshima bomb).

Range: Shorter than 1,000 kilometres. This is the definition set for inter-mediate-range missiles in the 1987 INF Treaty. However, precise range definitions are problematic - for example, an F16 plane with a non-strategic nuclear weapon has a range of almost 4,000 km.

Dual use: Unlike strategic nuclear weapons, almost all delivery vehicles (missiles, planes, artillery) for non-strategic nuclear weapons have dual, nuclear and conventional, uses. It is thus harder to monitor their use or deployment, relative to ICBMs or SLBMs.

Geography: It is hard to distinguish strategic from non-strategic weapons in the Middle East, South Asia and East Asia, given the short distances and the limited numbers of weapons.

For Russia, the initiative of 1991 also involved warheads for anti-aircraft missiles. Russia may have removed from deployment or destroyed up to 17,000 nuclear weapons. In October 1991, the United Kingdom decided to remove 200 nuclear bombs from ships and planes, and France gradually phased out its short-range ballistic missiles with nuclear warheads.

Thus the situation today with regard to deployments of such weapons is far more positive than it was 10–15 years ago. Yet, the weapons could still be redeployed, a concern that could be alleviated by converting the Presidential Nuclear Initiatives into a legally binding agreement.

The US has reportedly decided that 580 operational B61 nuclear gravity bombs should be set aside for use by US and NATO aircraft and that more than 400 of these are authorized for deployment at eight US airbases in six NATO countries. Russia has always reacted strongly against them saying that, given the range of NATO aircraft, their effects may be comparable to strategic nuclear weapons.

Political movements and non-governmental organizations in some European countries have argued that these so-called non-strategic nuclear weapons should be withdrawn. Contrary to claims long made by the United States and some other states, it is hard to believe that NATO would not retain relevance for its member states even if bombers deployed at NATO airbases by the US stop carrying nuclear weapons. NATO has already undertaken not to deploy such weapons in Central Europe in peacetime and certain NATO states have long refused any stationing of nuclear weapons on their territories.

Like NATO during the Cold War, Russia has come to place greater reliance on its large number of non-strategic nuclear weapons as a counter-weight to its perceived conventional military weakness vis-à-vis NATO. At the same time, Russia has held out the possibility of talks about removing these weapons, repeating its precondition that all states possessing such weapons should deploy them only on their own territory, implying that US weapons should be withdrawn from Europe.

In fact, retaining non-strategic nuclear weapons in Europe may be moti-vated on NATO's part by uncertainty over the future evolution of Russian domestic and foreign policies. Russia's deployments of such weapons appear motivated by concern over NATO's expansion to the east and its worldwide

---

BOX 13

SOME PROBLEMS WITH NON-STRATEGIC NUCLEAR WEAPONS

Numbers: Non-strategic nuclear weapons exist in large numbers. At the end of the Cold War, the Soviet Union reportedly had almost 22,000 war-heads for non-strategic weapons and the US had 5,000-6,000 warheads. Today Russia has 3,000-4,000 operational weapons and the US has about 2,100. Many weapons withdrawn from deployment are only stored and could be reintroduced.

Diversion risk: This is a serious problem with such weapons, which were designed to be used on the battlefield. They are generally smaller and more robust than strategic weapons and their security and safety system, or permissive-action link, may be less advanced than for a strategic weapon. This means that they would be easier for outsiders to use, such as a terrorist group. There is a risk of theft or diversion during transport or storage in the field.

Lack of a regime: The Presidential Nuclear Initiatives (1991/1992) are uni-lateral declarations by Russia and the US. There is no verification, no trans-parency and no legal commitment.

military operations. The Commission views the risks of future NATO-Russian political controversies as an additional reason to remove such weapons from operational deployment on European soil.

WMDC RECOMMENDATION

21 Russia and the United States should proceed to implement the commitments they made in 1991 to eliminate specific types of non-strategic nuclear weapons, such as demolition munitions, artillery shells and warheads for short-range ballistic missiles. They should agree to withdraw all non-strategic nuclear weapons to central storage on national territory, pending their eventual elimination. The two countries should reinforce their 1991 unilateral reduction commitments by developing arrangements to ensure verification, transparency and irreversibility.

WMDC RECOMMENDATION

22 Every state that possesses nuclear weapons should make a commitment not to deploy any nuclear weapon, of any type, on foreign soil.

Development of new nuclear weapons

The possibility of developing new types of nuclear weapons has been explored in the United States. Similar activities may be under way in other states, notably China and Russia. US advocates of new so-called low-yield weapons (often called mini-nukes) claim that such weapons would serve to deter other countries from seeking or using WMD. The Commission believes that developing such weapons, especially those with a lower threshold for use, would provide more of an inducement to other countries to do the same than a deterrent to proliferation. They would also be inconsistent with commitments made to strive for disarmament.

Many in the US Congress appear to share such concerns. In late 2005, for the second consecutive year, Congress denied the Administration's request for funding of the Robust Nuclear Earth Penetrator, also known as the 'bunker buster'. Congress also denied the Administration's request for funds to shorten the time to conduct nuclear tests from 24 months to 18 months. While Congress almost tripled (from $9 million to $25 million) the Administration's request for funding the Reliable Replacement Warhead

(RRW) programme, it also more than doubled (from $25 million to $60 million) the Administration's request for warhead dismantlement, underscoring 'the importance of an aggressive warhead dismantlement program'.

While many of these are welcome developments, it is likely that efforts will continue in several countries to find replacements for existing nuclear weapons and to upgrade such weapons, at least for safety and physical security purposes. The NPT nuclear-weapon states have an obligation vis-à-vis all states that have voluntarily forsworn nuclear weapons not to develop nuclear weapons with new military capabilities or for new missions. Of particular concern would be the adoption of doctrines and weapon systems that blur the distinction between nuclear and conventional weapons, or lower the nuclear threshold. Such modifications could over time have a domino effect and give rise to a renewed demand to resume nuclear testing. If research on nuclear weapons is continued, modifications should only be for purposes of safety and security – and demonstrably so.

WMDC RECOMMENDATION

23 Any state contemplating replacement or modernization of its nuclear-weapon systems must consider such action in the light of all relevant treaty obligations and its duty to contribute to the nuclear disarmament process. As a minimum, it must refrain from developing nuclear weapons with new military capabilities or for new missions. It must not adopt systems or doctrines that blur the distinction between nuclear and conventional weapons or lower the nuclear threshold.

Disposal of fissile material from warheads

The technical process of disarmament involves various risks to the environment, health and safety, if the dangerous materials are not properly handled. It is also very costly. Many of the risks relate to weapons-usable fissile material in nuclear arsenals or other such material in the civilian sector (see Box 14).

States dismantling nuclear weapons should dispose of the fissile material from warheads safely, securely, and in ways that exclude re-use in weapons. The most desirable solution is the destruction of the material or its conversion into a form not usable in weapons. It could be used for peaceful purposes as fuel or be placed in permanent storage, such as in geological repositories.

BOX 14

FISSILE MATERIAL CHALLENGES

A nuclear explosion results from the energy released as atoms of fissile material are split in a sudden chain reaction. The IAEA has set 8 kilograms of plutonium and 25 kilograms of highly enriched uranium as 'significant quantities' that should be detected by safeguards, although nuclear weapons can be made with less.

Civilian and military stocks of plutonium and highly enriched uranium each consists of nearly 2,000 metric tonnes (see table). Although most states possessing nuclear weapons have stated that they have stopped producing such material for weapons, some states produce or use such material for civilian purposes. Highly enriched uranium is used in some research reactors, various oceanic vessels for civilian and military uses, and the production of medical isotopes. Some states use plutonium in nuclear fuel.

Global Supplies of Fissile Material*

Type of use	Plutonium	Highly enriched uranium	Total
Civilian	1,700	175	1,875
Military	155	1,725	1,880
Total (metric tonnes)	**1,855**	**1,900**	**3,755**

Fissile material is difficult to produce. It requires more than mastering lab-scale fuel cycle processes. Outside the eight states that have nuclear weapons (nine if North Korea is included), only a few states possess the industrial installations to produce significant amounts of enriched uranium: Brazil, Germany, Japan and the Netherlands (Urenco). Japan is the only state outside the nuclear-weapon club that engages in industrial-scale reprocessing.

* From D. Albright and K. Kramer, *Bulletin of the Atomic Scientists* (November/December 2004).

In 1993, the United States and Russia concluded a bilateral agreement under which Russia would convert 500 tonnes of highly enriched uranium into low-enriched uranium for use in nuclear power plants in the United States. As of 30 June 2005, about half of that material had been converted. In 2000, the countries signed the Russian-US Plutonium Disposition Agreement, under which each state committed to what the White House called the 'safe, transparent, and irreversible disposition' of 68 metric tonnes of plutonium, with 34 tonnes coming from each country.

The pace of the conversion, especially the plutonium, has been slowed due to a variety of factors, such as lack of financial support, bureaucratic delays, secrecy and legal disputes. The rate of conversion and peaceful use of the uranium is also limited by market considerations. To increase the pace of the reduction of stocks of highly enriched uranium, states possessing such stocks should sell uranium blended to enrichment levels suitable for reactor fuel to other NPT states or use it for their own civil nuclear energy needs.

International expectations

The US and Russia have yet to implement the Trilateral Initiative – an undertaking launched in 1996 involving the US, Russia and the IAEA, to identify practical means by which redundant fissile material could be placed under IAEA safeguards without compromising the security of weapon designs or generating new proliferation risks. This initiative has still not been implemented due to unresolved issues regarding scope, duration and cost. Neither state has yet placed any of its warhead material under safeguards pursuant to this specific initiative.

Another step is for all nuclear-weapon states to place, as soon as practicable, fissile material designated by each of them as no longer required for military purposes under IAEA or other relevant international verification and make arrangements for the disposition of such material for peaceful purposes to ensure that such material remains permanently outside military programmes.

Concrete steps by these two nuclear-weapon states to implement the Trilateral Initiative and related efforts would help to show their determination to fulfil their disarmament commitments. Further delays would only send the opposite signal.

The United States has unilaterally placed under safeguards some fissile material that it has deemed to be in excess of its military needs, as has the United Kingdom. In October 2005, the United States announced that it would reserve up to 17 tonnes of highly enriched uranium to help establish a safeguarded fuel reserve to support nuclear-fuel assurances. A month later, it revealed plans to remove 200 metric tonnes of highly enriched uranium from its nuclear-weapon stockpile, most of which would be used for non-explosive military purposes (in naval propulsion systems).[3]

Irreversibility

One of the greatest challenges for achieving nuclear disarmament relates to the problem of ensuring that a state will not renege on its commitments and

3. Address of US Energy Secretary Sam Bodman, 2005 Carnegie International Nonproliferation Conference, Washington, D.C., 7 November 2005.

build or re-build a nuclear arsenal, a problem often called 'break-out'. The seriousness of this challenge was recognized at the 2000 NPT Review Conference. Since nuclear weapons cannot be made without fissile material, the international community has long attached great importance to ensuring the strictest of controls over all fissile material. This would require controls over both material recovered from warheads and weapons-usable fissile material in the civilian sector.

Irreversibility is difficult to achieve. However, in 1994 the US National Academy of Sciences proposed two standards to apply to the disposal of excess plutonium recovered from nuclear weapons. The first – a stored-weapon standard – held that excess weapons plutonium should be handled under controls 'approximating as closely as practicable the security and accounting applied to intact nuclear weapons'. The second – a spent-fuel standard – sought to protect against the reversibility of disarmament by ensuring that excess weapons plutonium would be made as inaccessible for weapons use as the plutonium in spent fuel.[4] In the Commission's view, these are reasonable standards to apply to all weapons-usable fissile material.

WMDC RECOMMENDATION

24
All states possessing nuclear weapons, notably Russia and the United States, should place their excess fissile material from military programmes under International Atomic Energy Agency safeguards. To facilitate the reduction of stocks of highly enriched uranium, states possessing such stocks should sell uranium blended to enrichment levels suitable for reactor fuel to other Non-Proliferation Treaty states or use it for their own peaceful nuclear energy needs.

WMDC RECOMMENDATION

25
All states possessing nuclear weapons should adopt strict standards for the handling of weapons-usable fissile material deemed excess to military requirements or recovered from disarmament activities, as exemplified in the US stored-weapon and spent-fuel standards.

---

4. National Academy of Sciences, Committee on International Security and Arms Control, 'Management and Disposition of Excess Weapons Plutonium' (Washington, D.C.: National Academies Press, 1994), p. 147.

Ending production of weapons-usable fissile material:
a fissile material cut-off treaty

Prohibition of the production of fissile material for use in nuclear weapons has long had broad support in the world community. It was included as a goal in the package deal that led to the indefinite extension of the NPT in 1995. The 2000 NPT Review Conference also endorsed it, as have several UN General Assembly resolutions. In 1995, the Conference on Disarmament agreed on a negotiation mandate for such a prohibition. However, there have been a number of difficulties that have so far prevented the CD from producing such a treaty.

The basic rationale for an FMCT is simple: while not alone sufficient to bring about disarmament, ending such production would at least halt the fresh supply of plutonium and highly enriched uranium for weapons. Closing the taps should not, in principle, be too difficult to achieve. Of the five NPT nuclear-weapon states, only China has not yet officially declared that it is no longer producing such material for weapons and should do so without delay. An FMCT also serves important non-proliferation and counter-terrorist goals by limiting the size of nuclear arsenals and by reducing the risk that fissile material for weapons could be diverted or stolen. Moreover, by applying to enrichment and reprocessing plants in both nuclear-weapon and non-nuclear-weapon states, it would remove an element of discrimination between the two categories of states.

While virtually all states find an FMCT desirable, difficulties remain.

Stocks. Even if fresh production of fissile material for weapons were to be stopped, states could still make new weapons from stockpiled fissile material. Because such stocks are quite large in some states, particularly in the United States and Russia, many non-nuclear-weapon states have maintained that the treaty should cover such stocks. Others, including the nuclear-weapon states, oppose this idea and want to confine the treaty to future production – a cut-off but not a cut-back. Special regional interests contribute to shaping the attitudes of many states in this matter. Pakistan and Arab states in the Middle East want stocks to be included, while India and some other states do not.

Verification has also become a controversial issue. The world community long ago appreciated the importance of verifying any agreement to prohibit the production of fissile material for weapons. Without verification, the world would have little assurance that the production of fissile material for weapons had in fact ceased. With little controversy, participants at the NPT Review Conferences in 1995 and 2000 endorsed the goal of negotiating an

FMCT with verification. While verification would require that all enrichment and reprocessing plants in states parties to the treaty, including nuclear-weapon states, would be subject to safeguards, this was thought doable and desirable. There are, in fact, rather few such plants. Such international verification is performed by the IAEA in some non-nuclear-weapon states parties to the NPT: Brazil, Germany, Japan and the Netherlands. It is further carried out in two nuclear-weapon states, France and the United Kingdom, pursuant to their Euratom and IAEA safeguards agreements.

However, can verification determine with a high degree of confidence that no fissile material usable for weapons is diverted from industrial-scale installations handling large volumes of such material? This and other difficulties, although recognized, are not seen by most states as insuperable, and the view dominates that an FMCT without verification would be of very limited value, if not damaging. Nevertheless, in July 2004, after having supported verification as a key element in an FMCT, the US reversed its policy and declared that 'realistic, effective verification of an FMCT is not achievable'. This position is rejected by a large number of states.

The Commission notes that, although the safeguarding of enrichment plants in non-nuclear-weapon states has long been recognized as posing special problems, practical solutions were found and were accepted by all members of the IAEA. The solutions were used in plants in Brazil, Japan and South Africa. The Agency thus has long experience of verifying the peaceful use of such installations. It is true that under an FMCT inspection of all the world's enrichment and reprocessing plants, including those in states that have nuclear weapons, would place a substantial additional workload on the Agency, especially if civilian nuclear power were to expand. But such an expansion will take place only over a long period of time, allowing for a gradual increase in the IAEA inspection capacity. The acceptance of IAEA verification of fuel-cycle plants in nuclear-weapon states on a voluntary basis would provide both the Agency and these states experience that would be useful in any future agreements on disarmament.

The road ahead. The vast majority of the world's countries continue to support verification as a part of an FMCT and view with scepticism an unverified cut-off. The Commission shares this scepticism. Indeed, such a construction would mirror one of the unequal features of the NPT – non-nuclear-weapon states must submit all their fuel-cycle activities to safeguards while nuclear-weapon states have no such obligation.

To overcome the differences over verification, and the question relating to the status of stocks of fissile materials, these issues could be examined on their merits in the course of future negotiations. In addition, either as preparation for the negotiations or in parallel with them, a Group of Scientific Experts could be set up in the Conference on Disarmament, as was done before the CTBT negotiations, which would be charged with examining technical questions, including such issues as the scope of the materials to be covered by such a treaty and the specific measures that would enhance confidence in the verification process. In the next few years much experience will be gained by the IAEA regarding inspection of both enrichment and reprocessing plants, especially in Japan. Further valuable experience could be gained if in the same period nuclear-weapon states would voluntarily submit such plants to inspection.

WMDC RECOMMENDATION

26 The Conference on Disarmament should immediately open the delayed negotiations for a treaty on the cut-off of production of fissile material for weapons without preconditions. Before, or at least during, these negotiations, the Conference on Disarmament should establish a Group of Scientific Experts to examine technical aspects of the treaty.

WMDC RECOMMENDATION

27 To facilitate fissile material cut-off negotiations in the Conference on Disarmament, the five Non-Proliferation Treaty nuclear-weapon states, joined by the other states possessing nuclear weapons, should agree among themselves to cease production of fissile material for weapon purposes. They should open up their facilities for such production to International Atomic Energy Agency safeguards inspections, building on the practice of Euratom inspections in France and the UK. These eight states should also address the issue of verifiable limitations of existing stocks of weapons-usable nuclear materials.

Ending all nuclear-weapon tests: the Comprehensive Nuclear-Test-Ban Treaty

Test explosions are a key step in the design, development and refinement of nuclear weapons. They have also been widely regarded as a political message: a signal to the outside world that a country has mastered the technology of nuclear weapons.

BOX 15

NUCLEAR-WEAPON TESTS BY THE FIVE NPT
NUCLEAR-WEAPON STATES, INDIA AND PAKISTAN

Country	Latest	In the atmosphere or under water	Underground	Total
USA	1992	217	815	1,032
Soviet Union	1990	219	496	715
France	1996	50	160	210
UK	1991	21	24	45
China	1996	23	22	45
India	1998	--	3	3
Pakistan	1998	--	2	2
Total		**530**	**1,522**	**2,052**

Source: *SIPRI Yearbook 1998*, Appendix 12B, pp. 562–563.
(Note: SIPRI uses the definition of a nuclear test found in the Threshold Test-Ban Treaty, which counts as a single event simultaneous tests of nuclear devices at a specific location.)

The adherence of all states to the Comprehensive Nuclear-Test-Ban Treaty would serve several vital objectives. First of all, it would prevent or inhibit qualitative improvements in existing weapons. Second, all non-nuclear-weapon states parties to the NPT would become participants in the global verification system of the treaty and would be formal stakeholders in the treaty. Third, universal support of the CTBT, bringing the treaty into force and operation, would send a strong signal that all the states of the world are once again on the path to disarmament.

For over half a century the international community has sought an end to nuclear testing. In the early 1950s public concern was aroused as a result of both radioactive fall-out from atmospheric nuclear tests and worries about the escalating nuclear arms race.

In the years following the first nuclear test, conducted in July 1945, more than 2,000 nuclear test explosions were conducted, initially in the atmosphere and under water, later underground, mostly by the United States and the Soviet Union, but also by France, China and the United Kingdom (see Box 15). The NPT nuclear-weapon states have not conducted any nuclear tests since the CTBT was opened for signature in September 1996. The most recent tests were conducted by France and China in 1996 and India and Pakistan in 1998.

Several international instruments and many UN General Assembly resolutions underline the need for a comprehensive test ban. The Preamble of the

Partial Test-Ban Treaty (PTBT) refers to the goal of 'seeking to achieve the discontinuance of all test explosions of nuclear weapons for all time' and 'to continue negotiations to this end'. One of the key components of the package deal that led to the indefinite extension of the NPT in 1995 was a call for the completion of negotiations on a CTBT by 1996. While the CTBT was in fact adopted by the UN General Assembly and opened for signature in September 1996, it has still not entered into force.

Obstacles to entry into force. When the CTBT was opened for signature in 1996, it was signed by 71 states, including the five NPT nuclear-weapon states. As of April 2006, the number of signatories has grown to 176 states, with 132 ratifications. However, the treaty will only enter into force 180 days after 44 designated states involved in nuclear activities have ratified it.

Of these 44 states, only 34 have ratified it so far. Among the ten that have not, seven states – China, Colombia, Egypt, Indonesia, Iran, Israel and the United States – have signed but not ratified it. Three states have neither signed nor ratified the treaty: India, North Korea and Pakistan.

President Bill Clinton was the first leader to sign the CTBT in 1996. However, the US Senate refused in 1999 to provide its consent to ratification. The present US administration does not support the treaty and will not seek its ratification. Yet it has declared that it would continue to observe the 1992 unilateral moratorium on such tests. Although neither India nor Pakistan has signed either the NPT or the CTBT, they have both committed themselves not to carry out further nuclear tests.

The Commission believes that a US decision to ratify the CTBT would strongly influence other countries to follow suit. It would decisively improve the chances for entry into force of the treaty and would have more positive ramifications for arms control and disarmament than any other single measure. While no nuclear-weapon tests have been carried out for many years, leaving the treaty in limbo is a risk to the whole international community. The United States should reconsider its position and proceed to ratify the treaty. Only the CTBT offers the prospect of a permanent and legally binding commitment to end nuclear testing.

The global verification regime of the CTBT is already partly operational. It comprises facilities for seismological, hydro-acoustic, infrasound and radio-nuclide monitoring, including a network of 321 monitoring stations and 16 radionuclide laboratories. Over 100 stations are already transmitting data. However, the CTBT Organization (CTBTO) has had difficulties collecting the annual dues owed to the organization. Although political support for the CTBT remains strong, ensuring continuous financing for the verification system remains a major challenge. The Commission considers the monitoring system to be essential to the continued credibility of the CTBT and encourages all signatories to support it politically and financially.

WMDC RECOMMENDATION

28 All states that have not already done so should sign and ratify the Comprehensive Nuclear-Test-Ban Treaty unconditionally and without delay. The United States, which has not ratified the treaty, should reconsider its position and proceed to ratify the treaty, recognizing that its ratification would trigger other required ratifications and be a step towards the treaty's entry into force. Pending entry into force, all states with nuclear weapons should continue to refrain from nuclear testing. Also, the 2007 conference of Comprehensive Nuclear-Test-Ban Treaty signatories should address the possibility of a provisional entry into force of the treaty.

WMDC RECOMMENDATION

29 All signatories should provide financial, political and technical support for the continued development and operation of the verification regime, including the International Monitoring System, the International Data Centre and the secretariat, so that the CTBTO is ready to monitor and verify compliance with the treaty when it enters into force. They should pledge to maintain their respective stations and continue to transmit data on a national basis under all circumstances.

FROM REGULATING NUCLEAR WEAPONS TO OUTLAWING THEM

Nuclear weapons must never again be used – by states or by terrorists – and the only way to be sure of that is to get rid of them before someone, somewhere is tempted to use them.

Today, we are in a dangerous situation. There has been a third wave of nuclear proliferation. Proliferation has not been halted and serious steps to outlaw nuclear weapons have not been taken.

---

5. President Reagan's Second Inaugural Address, Monday, 21 January 1985.

President Ronald Reagan said in his second inaugural address: 'We seek the total elimination one day of nuclear weapons from the face of the Earth'.[5] This was in 1985. The Commission concurs. Nuclear weapons are remnants of the Cold War. It is time to outlaw them, as the world has done in the case of chemical and biological weapons.

In a landmark advisory opinion, the International Court of Justice agreed unanimously that:

'There exists an obligation to pursue in good faith and bring to a conclusion negotiations leading to nuclear disarmament in all its aspects under strict and effective international control.'

Such an obligation requires that states actively pursue measures to reduce the numbers of nuclear weapons and the importance of their role in military force structures. Yet, even though nuclear-weapon states ask other states to plan for their security without nuclear weapons, they do not themselves seem to be planning for this eventuality.

A key challenge is to dispel the perception that outlawing nuclear weapons is a utopian goal. A nuclear disarmament treaty is achievable and can be reached through careful, sensible and practical measures. Benchmarks should be set; definitions agreed; timetables drawn up and agreed upon; and transparency requirements agreed. Disarmament work should be set in motion. This chapter identifies many measures and initiatives that would move the world towards nuclear disarmament. It is time to move from the present stalemate and revive the discussion and negotiations about such steps.

In 1956 President Dwight D. Eisenhower said:

'If men can develop weapons that are so terrifying as to make the thought of global war include almost a sentence for suicide, you would think that man's intelligence and his comprehension ... would include also his ability to find a peaceful solution.'[6]

The Commission believes that President Eisenhower was right.

WMDC RECOMMENDATION

30 All states possessing nuclear weapons should commence planning for security without nuclear weapons. They should start preparing for the outlawing of nuclear weapons through joint practical and incremental measures that include definitions, benchmarks and transparency requirements for nuclear disarmament.

---

6. President Dwight D. Eisenhower, Press Conference, Washington, D.C., 14 November 1956.

Biological and toxin weapons

Biological and toxin weapons

Biological warfare and bioterrorism involve the deliberate cause or spread of disease by biological agents, used as a weapon. Such weapons have the potential to cause immense human harm, panic and societal disruption. Although governments have long understood that eliminating the threats posed by these weapons will require extensive international cooperation, the need for such cooperation is more urgent today than ever.

This urgency arises from several converging developments. One concerns the rapid evolution in the life sciences, with possibly unforeseen, dangerous consequences. Another is that the 1972 Biological and Toxin Weapons Convention lacks a capacity for monitoring and verification, implementation and enforcement. An additional problem is that many governments have not adopted or fully implemented national legislation and other instruments to ensure fulfilment of their obligations. Yet another concern arises from the possible misuse or negative impact of biodefence programmes, such as their potential to provide cover for the illegal development or maintenance of biological weapons-related expertise. Furthermore, there is a heightened fear of the impact of terrorist actions, coupled with profound concern that modern economies may be particularly vulnerable to disruption from the deliberate spread of disease.

The Commission recognizes that strengthening the prohibition embodied in the BTWC is a necessary, but not sufficient, requirement for dealing with these intractable, interrelated problems.

In view also of the potentially rising threat posed by the acquisition and use by terrorists of these weapons, there is a growing need for the public to be better informed. People need to be aware not only of the risks, but also about what to do in an emergency. This will require striking a delicate balance between the public's legitimate right to know and the duty to minimize the risk of causing collective disruption or panic.

One problem is that most biological agents that have the potential to be used as weapons also exist in nature. Thus it may be difficult in the early stages

Biological weapons can be subdivided in several ways. One way is to consider the *type of agent* that causes disease, such as bacteria, viruses or toxins. Another is to look at the *types of effects*, such as a disease that can be transmitted between humans (contagious) or only affects those directly exposed to the biological agent. A third way is to look at *symptoms* – for example, some diseases might normally lead to death while others might incapacitate their victims or lead to changes in behaviour.

of an outbreak to determine whether a disease has been deliberately induced or has occurred naturally. While the immediate priority following the outbreak of disease will be to respond quickly to mitigate its effects, both governments and the public need to know whether this is a natural occurrence or a man-made one for which the perpetrators must be found.

In the 21st century, the ever-expanding global transport of goods and livestock, and the growth in international travel, mean that an outbreak of a highly contagious disease in one place could quickly spread around the world. Inevitably, scientific advancements in biotechnology and the wide spread of facilities capable of producing biological agents make it exceedingly difficult to pinpoint potential biological threats.

PROHIBITION OF BIOLOGICAL WEAPONS

The use of poisonous substances as weapons of war was prohibited before World War I. Nevertheless, poisonous gas was used extensively in that war. This caused such abhorrence that the international community decided to prohibit the use of both chemical and biological weapons in war. The Protocol for the Prohibition of the Use in War of Asphyxiating, Poisonous or Other Gases and of Bacteriological Methods of Warfare (the Geneva Protocol) was signed in 1925 and entered into force in 1928 (see Box 17). The Protocol bans the use – but not the production, stockpiling or deployment – of such weapons.

Many states reserved the right to retaliate in kind if attacked with the prohibited weapons. Although the norm held for most of World War II, biological weapons were used by the Japanese military in attacks and experiments conducted against wartime opponents. During the war, other states also conducted biological warfare research. After World War II, a number of biological warfare research programmes were undertaken, the largest of which

THE GENEVA PROTOCOL

Protocol for the Prohibition of the Use in War of Asphyxiating Gas, and of
Bacteriological Methods of Warfare

Signed on 17 June 1925 and entered into force on 8 February 1928

- Prohibits the use in war of asphyxiating, poisonous or other gases, and of
  all analogous liquids, materials or devices
- Prohibits the use of bacteriological methods of warfare
- Commits the parties to exert every effort to induce other States to accede

*The prohibitions 'shall be universally accepted as a part of International
Law, binding alike the conscience and the practice of nations'.*

were conducted by the Soviet Union and the United States – the diseases that were made to be used as weapons included anthrax, smallpox, plague and tularaemia.

The Convention on the Prohibition of the Development, Production and Stockpiling of Bacteriological (Biological) and Toxin Weapons and on Their Destruction (BTWC) was signed in 1972 and entered into force in 1975. The BTWC bans the development, production, stockpiling and acquisition of biological and toxin weapons and requires the destruction or conversion of such weapons or delivery means. The Convention embodies the principle known as the general purpose criterion under which all relevant activities are prohibited unless they can be justified for the peaceful purposes permitted under the Convention, including justifications relating to types and quantities of materials being used for prophylactic, protective or other peaceful purposes.

The BTWC (as of April 2006) has 155 parties – fewer than either the NPT or the CWC. A further 16 states have signed but not ratified the Convention, while more than 20 states have neither signed nor ratified it (see Box 18). In order for the overall regime to be strengthened the parties need to promote universal adherence to the Convention.

The BTWC has no provision for the formal monitoring or verification of compliance or implementation. Unlike the CWC, there is no central institution or verification regime for the BTWC.

Widespread concern about how confidence in compliance with the BTWC could be enhanced led the BTWC parties to convene in 1991 an Ad Hoc Group of Governmental Experts to Identify and Examine Potential Verification Measures from a Scientific and Technical Standpoint (VEREX). The final report of VEREX, with recommendations, was presented to a Special Conference of

BTWC states parties in 1994. This conference agreed to develop a legally binding instrument to strengthen the effectiveness and improve the implementation of the BTWC.

Negotiations on a verification protocol began in 1995 and continued through 2001, when they were brought to a sudden halt by the withdrawal of the support of the United States. The 2001 Review Conference had to be suspended. By the time it reconvened in 2002 it was clear that the draft verification protocol, at least as negotiated, would go no further without support from the US. The Review Conference was able only to adopt a decision to hold annual expert and political meetings of states parties until the end of 2006, when the Sixth Review Conference is to be held.

As mentioned above, a significant development was the adoption in 2004 by the UN Security Council of Resolution 1540, which is binding on all UN member states. It reaffirms the need for all states to fulfil their obligations in relation to arms control and disarmament and to prevent proliferation in all its aspects of all weapons of mass destruction. The resolution requires all states to 'adopt and enforce appropriate effective laws which prohibit any non-state actor to manufacture, acquire, possess, develop, transport, transfer or use nuclear, chemical or biological weapons or their means of delivery' and to 'enforce effective measures to establish domestic controls' to prevent their proliferation. This in effect enhances Article IV of the BTWC, which calls on states parties to prohibit the acquisition of biological weapons by any person under their jurisdiction or control.

PROSPECTS FOR THE FUTURE

Strengthening the role of the Convention

The biological threat poses multifaceted challenges and requires multifaceted solutions. So far, however, there is scant agreement on how to move forward. Some states have abandoned any hope of strengthening international confidence in compliance. Some are still seeking to revive the idea of the verification protocol. Others now want to move on and build bridges between collective, treaty-based mechanisms and other approaches.

In the Commission's view, efforts to achieve some level of multilaterally agreed principles and powers should be pursued, although the complexities of the challenge make it necessary to counter biological-weapon threats from a variety of angles. The international community should focus simultaneously

on the following types of activity, all of which contribute to the overall regime
for control of the hostile uses of the life sciences.

- strengthening and effective enforcement of international agreements,
  including monitoring and reporting
- increasing public health awareness combined with enhanced health and
  safety regulations, measures and resources
- controls on transfers of material and equipment
- norm building among all those engaged in the life sciences and in society
  as a whole
- public information
- counter-terrorism intelligence and tools.

Although a number of different solutions have been proposed, states have
failed to address the complete range of possibilities in the context of the
current series of annual meetings of the BTWC states parties. Some of the
solutions that have been proposed are for strengthening the UN's verification
capacities, either directly associated with the BTWC or as part of an effort to
build on the lessons and institutional capabilities of UNMOVIC. Others focus
on developing codes of conduct, ethics and accounting for scientific and medical activities, strengthening the capability of health systems to discover and
treat the spread of disease, as well as increasing worldwide awareness of the
dangers of biological attack by means of a public information campaign.

A multifaceted approach is required – one that strengthens the multilateral normative and legal prohibition regime, while linking it with other
kinds of governmental and non-governmental, national and international
measures. The nuclear and chemical industries cooperate actively with
governments and have found this to be in their interest. Bioindustry can and
should do likewise. It has much to gain in credibility and respectability by
cooperating in preventing abuse of biotechnology, as the nuclear and chemical industries have in their respective fields. However, a key to progress
worldwide would be for the US to commit itself actively to international
approaches and instruments.

Despite its shortcomings – the lack of verification arrangements and permanent institutional support – the BTWC remains the only multilateral treaty
with a broad consensus that provides an international standard by which
biological activities can be judged.

The last full review of the operation of the BTWC was in 1991. In view of
developments since then, the parties need to carry out a full review during the
2006 Review Conference. It is crucially important for the BTWC states par-

NON-PARTIES TO THE BTWC

States that have signed but not yet ratified:
Burundi, Central African Republic, Cote d'Ivoire, Egypt, Gabon, Guyana, Haiti, Liberia, Madagascar, Malawi, Myanmar, Nepal, Somalia, Syria, United Arab Emirates, Tanzania

Non-signatory states:
Andorra, Angola, Cameroon, Chad, Comoros, Cook Island, Djibouti, Eritrea, Guinea, Israel, Kazakhstan, Kiribati, Marshall Islands, Mauritius, Micronesia, Mozambique, Namibia, Nauru, Niue, Samoa, Trinidad and Tobago, Tuvalu, Zambia

ties to use the Sixth Review Conference, to be held in late 2006, to reassert the Convention's role as the central component of the overall regime and agree on concrete measures to implement it. The Commission's recommendations aim at making maximum use of this opportunity.

WMDC RECOMMENDATION

31 All states not yet party to the Biological and Toxin Weapons Convention should adhere to the Convention. The states parties to the Convention should launch a campaign to achieve universal adherence by the time of the Seventh Review Conference, to be held in 2011.

National implementation

There is a need to enhance national BTWC implementation, including the development of national legislation and enforcement procedures. Security Council Resolution 1540 requires that all states shall 'adopt and enforce appropriate effective laws which prohibit any non-state actor to manufacture, acquire, possess, develop, transport, transfer or use nuclear, chemical or biological weapons or their means of delivery' and 'enforce effective measures to establish domestic controls' to prevent their proliferation.

The effectiveness of the prohibitions of the BTWC depends on the full national implementation of the Convention through national legislation and regulations. Given the uneven level of activity and expertise among the BTWC states parties, interested governments should promote a network of designated national authorities or functional focal points. Such a network could coordinate implementation support and assistance. It could promote best-practice models for national legislation and training in the range of activities needed to ensure national compliance; it could share information to assist parties to comply with all their BTWC obligations; and it could serve as a clearing-house for technical assistance and advice.

Confidence-building measures (CBMs) can play an important role. The second BTWC Review Conference, held in 1986, agreed that parties should make annual declarations on various biological weapon-related matters in an effort to increase transparency and build confidence. These were revised and expanded in 1991, at the third Review Conference. However, participation in the CBMs has never been high and has been declining. The annual declarations are collated by the UN Department for Disarmament Affairs and distributed only to parties. (They can be made in national languages, and are not even translated.) So far, only three countries – Australia, the UK and the US – have made their declarations public. Given that the data are not publicly reviewed, little political attention is paid to them and states therefore have little incentive to report.

While CBMs increase transparency, they can in no sense be described as measures for monitoring or verification. However, they offer a way for states on their own initiative to promote and demonstrate effective implementation of the BTWC, thus adding to the impetus for multilateral verification. BTWC parties that wish to indicate their support for a multilateral verification system for the Convention could use the CBMs to demonstrate their commitment to reporting publicly the record of BTWC-relevant activities under their jurisdiction.

WMDC RECOMMENDATION

32 To achieve universal adoption of national legislation and regulations to implement the Biological and Toxin Weapons Convention completely and effectively, the states parties should offer technical assistance and promote best-practice models of such legislation. As a part of the confidence-building process and to promote transparency and harmonization, all states parties should make annual biological-weapon-related national declarations and make them public.

Institutional deficit

The BTWC has no standing institution to monitor and oversee compliance and implementation. Nor is any related monitoring institution able to perform the functions that the OPCW carries out for the CWC or that the IAEA performs for the NPT. Over the years there have been various attempts to address this institutional deficit. In addition to the formal negotiations in the 1990s for a BTWC protocol, these include: the use of the compliance consultation mechanism agreed by the 1996 Review Conference (and used to address a 1997 allegation by Cuba against the United States); the UN Secretary-General's mechanism to investigate allegations of breaches of the 1925 Geneva Protocol; confidence-building measures; and voluntary verification arrangements, most notably the short-lived US–UK–Russia trilateral initiative to investigate allegations about Soviet breaches of the BTWC.

WMDC RECOMMENDATION

33 States parties to the Biological and Toxin Weapons Convention should enhance the investigatory powers of the UN Secretary-General, ensuring that the Secretary-General's office can rely upon a regularly up-dated roster of experts and advice from the World Health Organization and a specialist unit, modelled on the United Nations Monitoring, Verification and Inspection Commission, to assist in investigating unusual outbreaks of disease and allegations of the use of biological weapons.

WMDC RECOMMENDATION

34 States parties to the Biological and Toxin Weapons Convention should establish a standing secretariat to handle organizational and administrative matters related to the treaty, such as Review Conferences and expert meetings.

Implementation of the Convention

States parties should also agree to consider ways and means to strengthen the effectiveness and improve the implementation of the BTWC by adopting a substantive programme of work for the five years following the 2006 Review Conference, starting with regular annual meetings from 2007. It is time for all states parties to make a fresh start and not be distracted by previous disagreements.

As noted above, nowadays the transport of goods and relative ease of international travel mean that an outbreak of a transmissible disease in one place could spread quickly throughout the world. Inevitably, scientific advancements in biotechnology and the widespread availability of facilities capable of producing biological agents make it more difficult to prevent the development of biological weapons and complicate efforts to ensure their non-production and the elimination of stocks.

The effects of biological weapons can be limited by putting in place measures for early discovery and for alerting the public quickly and effectively. In addition to the work of upgrading national and international public health systems, there needs to be a more effective system to enable containment or quarantine to be put into effect. Such practices made a difference in containing the SARS outbreak in 2003, but they need to be better coordinated internationally. More can also be done to exchange information and equip local health services with better training and resources, including vaccinations or other prophylactic measures.

At the same time, it must be recognized that, since biological weapons can be disseminated by means of air, food or water and it is not possible to predict where, when and with what a bioterrorist might strike, full protection is not possible to achieve. The point is to be as well prepared as possible. This calls for cooperation between civilian health and security-oriented authorities, nationally, regionally and worldwide. Such preparations will increase the chances of saving lives and limiting the effects of an attack, but enhanced education and health resources will be intrinsically valuable for individual countries and civil society. Raising public awareness will also help enhance the stigma attached to biological weapons, especially to their use by states.

Better preparedness may avert or reduce the effects of terrorist attacks. Therefore, there is a need to establish clear international standards for, and to jointly implement, the approaches that are particularly relevant for dealing with non-state (i.e. terrorist) menaces – better identification, consolidating and guarding of dangerous biomaterials, facilities and knowledge, plus urgent international cooperation to destroy left-over and unwanted stocks, coupled with better controls on the export and transit of related objects. (On these issues see also Chapter 7 of this report.)

In addition, all states should implement fully the new International Health Regulations that were adopted by the World Health Organization in May 2005; they comprise legally binding provisions for member states on sharing epidemiological information about health emergencies that could have international ramifications.

WMDC RECOMMENDATION

35 Governments should pursue public health surveillance to ensure effective monitoring of unusual outbreaks of disease and develop practical methods of coordinating international responses to any major event that might involve bioweapons. They should strengthen cooperation between civilian health and security-oriented author- ities, nationally, regionally and worldwide, including in the frame- work of the new International Health Regulations of the World Health Organization. Governments should also review their national biosafety and biosecurity measures to protect health and the envi- ronment from the release of biological and toxin materials. They should harmonize national biosecurity standards.

Life sciences and the role of scientists

Devising measures to strengthen individual responsibility in scientific research involves a delicate balance between the legitimate quest for new knowledge, especially in fields where advances can greatly enhance medical and other kinds of peaceful developments, and the dangers to society inher- ent in certain kinds of work.

Some projects of the Cooperative Threat Reduction programme have been directed towards retraining weapon scientists and, where possible, finding ways for their skills to be used in the service of non-proliferation and security.

In addition to transfer or export controls and supply-side restrictions on some activities or materials, which may also be necessary, there is a need for all countries and competent institutions to provide bioweapon awareness training for biologists and biotechnologists working in the public and private sectors. Specifically, two kinds of normative approach should be actively considered, separately or combined – a code of ethics and a code of conduct (this matter is currently examined in separate processes in the United Nations Educational, Scientific and Cultural Organization, UNESCO, and the Inter- national Committee of the Red Cross, ICRC). A code of ethics may be thought of as a short, generic, scientific Hippocratic oath whereby those engaged in the life sciences (on entry to higher-education science courses or on graduat- ing) pledge to use science only for the benefit of humanity. Codes of conduct or codes of practice, in contrast, are envisaged more as a professional guide to good practice that would be part of science education from secondary school to university and professional training, to raise awareness of the moral issues as well as instilling good practices for maintaining the security of materials, facilities and sensitive technologies. (On these issues see also Chapter 7 of this report.)

In 2003, the focus of the inter-sessional BTWC meetings was on the adoption of national implementation measures, including the enactment of penal legislation, and on the establishment and effective implementation of national mechanisms to maintain the security and oversight of pathogenic organisms and toxins. The 2004 meetings focused on enhancing international capabilities for responding to, investigating and mitigating suspected or actual BTWC threats or attacks. They also emphasized the need to strengthen and broaden national and international institutional efforts and mechanisms for surveillance, detection, diagnosis and the combating of infectious diseases that affect humans, animals or plants. They emphasized the importance of early detection and immediate and effective response, and they encouraged further cooperation between national institutions and emergency services and international organizations, such as the World Health Organization (WHO), the World Organisation for Animal Health (OIE) and the UN Food and Agriculture Organization (FAO). The 2005 meetings discussed the content, promulgation and adoption of codes of conduct for scientists.

The Sixth Review Conference, to be held later this year, is to assess the result of this work programme and decide on further action.

Potential problems may emanate from rapid developments in the life sciences, including new understandings of genes and proteins that could eventually outpace national and international efforts to prevent, control or manage the hostile uses of biology. In recent years, materials and technologies have become accessible to many more researchers and technicians through the pharmaceutical and biotechnology industries. In addition, there is the possibility that terrorists could recruit highly skilled scientists. This assessment has to be qualified, however: while it could be within the reach of a group of skilled biologists to concoct a lethal biological agent, it requires a different set of skills, expertise and equipment to weaponize it and to target and deliver it over a large population. There is little evidence that terrorist groups presently are capable of doing this.

WMDC RECOMMENDATION

36 At the Sixth Review Conference, in 2006, the states parties to the Biological and Toxin Weapons Convention should reaffirm common understandings reached at previous review conferences and take action on all subjects addressed at Convention meetings since 2003. They should also establish a work programme on additional topics for future meetings. States parties should ensure more frequent reassessment of the implications of scientific and technological developments and reaffirm that all undertakings under Article I of the Biological and Toxin Weapons Convention apply to such developments. This Review Conference should reaffirm that all developments in the life sciences fall within the scope of the Convention and that all developments in the life sciences for hostile purposes are prohibited by the Convention.

Chemical weapons

CHAPTER 5

Chemical weapons

The abhorrence of the use of 'poison' as a weapon has deep roots in history. The 1899 Hague Declaration prohibited the use of projectiles whose sole object was 'the diffusion of asphyxiating and deleterious gases'. The 1907 Hague Convention IV prohibited the use of 'poison and poisoned weapons'. Nevertheless, gas – most often mustard gas – was used extensively in World War I. The public was horrified. As a result, the Geneva Protocol (Protocol for the Prohibition of the Use in War of Asphyxiating, Poisonous or Other Gases, and of Bacteriological Methods of Warfare) was adopted in 1925.

The Geneva Protocol, while expanding the existing bans to cover also 'bacteriological' weapons, applied only to their *use*. It imposed no restriction on *development*, *production* and *stockpiling*. Many of the states that ratified the protocol expressly reserved the right to use the otherwise prohibited weapons against an enemy state not party to the Protocol, or – as retaliation

---

BOX 19

THE MAIN TYPES OF CHEMICAL WEAPONS:

Nerve agent: highly lethal, kills in very small dosages. E.g. sarin, soman, VX.

Blistering agent: causes burns and blisters on the body, damages eyes. If inhaled it severely damages the lungs, which often leads to death. E.g. mustard sulphurous gas, lewisite.

Asphyxiating agent: causes damage to the lungs. E.g. phosgene, mustard gas.

Psychotomimetic agent: causes a hallucinatory effect similar in kind to that of LSD. E.g. BZ.

Incapacitating agent: relies on irritants and toxic effects to incapacitate a person temporarily. Depending on purpose of use they might be allowed under the CWC. E.g. tear gas, CS.

Possible new agents: research on new ways of affecting the human brain to cause aggressiveness, sleepiness, fear or other emotions. E.g. bioregulators.

in kind – against a party using chemical weapons in violation of its obligations under the Protocol.

In the inter-war period, chemical weapons were used by Spain in Morocco, by Italy in Abyssinia and by Japan in China. In World War II, poisonous gases killed millions in Nazi concentration camps, and chemical weapons were used in Asia. But they were not used on European battlefields. Since the end of that war chemical weapons have been used by Egypt in North Yemen (1963–67); in the Iraq–Iran war (1980–88); and by the Iraqi Government against its own Kurdish civilian population. In the Vietnam War, defoliants and CS gas were used by the United States.

Although states have been the major users of chemical weapons, current concerns are primarily about the use of these weapons by terrorists.

THE CHEMICAL WEAPONS CONVENTION

After some 20 years of negotiations, a complete ban on the development, production, stockpiling and use of chemical weapons finally came into effect in 1997, when the Chemical Weapons Convention (CWC) entered into force.

There are 178 parties to the CWC as of April 2006. Containing extensive

---

BOX 20

DEFINITION OF CHEMICAL WEAPONS (CWC ARTICLE II):

1. 'Chemical Weapons' means the following, together or separately:
(a) Toxic chemicals and their precursors, except where intended for purposes not prohibited under this Convention, as long as the types and quantities are consistent with such purposes;
(b) Munitions and devices, specifically designed to cause death or other harm through the toxic properties of those toxic chemicals specified in subparagraph (a), which would be released as a result of the employment of such munitions and devices;
(c) Any equipment specifically designed for use directly in connection with the employment of munitions and devices specified in subparagraph (b).

2. 'Toxic Chemical' means:
Any chemical, which through its chemical action on life processes can cause death, temporary incapacitation or permanent harm to humans or animals. This includes all such chemicals, regardless of their origin or of their method of production, and regardless of whether they are produced in facilities, in munitions or elsewhere.

BOX 21

WHICH CHEMICALS ARE CONTROLLED?

Schedule 1 chemicals include those that have been or can easily be used as chemical weapons and which have very limited, if any, uses for peaceful purposes. These chemicals are subject to very stringent restrictions, including ceilings on production (1 tonne per annum per state party) and possession, licensing requirements and restrictions on transfers. These restrictions apply to the relatively few industrial facilities that use such chemicals. Some of these chemicals are used as ingredients in pharmaceutical preparations or as diagnostics. Others are produced and used for protective purposes, such as for testing CW protective equipment and chemical agent alarms.

Schedule 2 chemicals include those that are precursors to, or that in some cases can themselves be used as, chemical weapon agents, but which have a number of other commercial uses (such as ingredients in resins, flame-retardants, additives, inks and dyes, insecticides, herbicides, lubricants and some raw materials for pharmaceutical products).

Schedule 3 chemicals include those that can be used to produce, or can be used as, chemical weapons, but which are widely used for peaceful purposes (including plastics, resins, mining chemicals, petroleum refining fumigants, paints, coatings, anti-static agents and lubricants).

Discrete Organic Chemicals (DOCs) are among those chemicals not specifically listed in the Schedules or anywhere in the Convention. Manufacturing operations producing DOCs are referred to as 'other chemical production facilities'. These plant sites are subject to declarations and verification requirements if they produce in aggregate more than 200 tonnes of DOCs annually. They are also subject to these requirements if they comprise plants at which more than 30 tonnes of any DOCs containing the elements phosphorous, sulphur or fluorine (PSF chemicals) are produced. Thousands of plant sites have been declared to the OPCW.

verification measures, the CWC requires states parties to declare and then to destroy all stocks of chemical weapons within 10 years of entry into force (by 2007), with a possible extension of up to five years (by 2012). Most importantly, the Convention completely prohibits their future development, production, stockpiling, transfer and use.

Unlike the NPT, which allows five states to retain nuclear weapons, all rules in the CWC are non-discriminatory. They apply equally to all its parties, whether they are great powers or small. Another important difference between the treaties is that, unlike the NPT, the CWC establishes well-

THE CWC IMPLEMENTATION AND INSPECTION BODY

The Organisation for the Prohibition of Chemical Weapons (OPCW), based in The Hague, monitors the implementation of the CWC. The OPCW has a staff of fewer than 500, including some 180 inspectors who are trained and equipped to inspect military and industry facilities in member states. By April 2006, OPCW inspection teams had carried out over 2,300 inspections at more than 700 sites in 74 countries.

defined authorities – a Conference of the States Parties, an Executive Council and a Technical Secretariat – to be responsible for the operation and implementation of the Convention.

The comprehensive prohibition of the acquisition, production and use of chemical weapons has been a success. However, a number of challenges remain. They are listed in one document and two plans of action that were adopted by the 2003 CWC Review Conference. The problems, which are addressed below, include:

- A failure to meet CWC deadlines for destruction of chemical weapon stocks
- Several states still have not joined the CWC
- A continued interest among states in the development of non-lethal chemical weapons, such as incapacitants
- Shortcomings in verification and inspection activities
- Limited applicability to non-state actors (terrorists)
- Uneven implementation among state parties

Destroying the chemical-weapon stockpiles

Only the complete destruction of all stockpiles of chemical weapons will ensure that these weapons cannot be used by states or terrorist groups and that there can be no accidental releases. The CWC requires that states declare and then destroy their stockpiles by 2007 in accordance with an agreed schedule. However, a major problem in the implementation of the CWC has been and remains the slow rate of destruction of the vast chemical weapon arsenals built up by the United States and the Soviet Union during the Cold War, as well as of those abandoned by Japan in China during World War II. The high cost of destruction and the environmental and safety concerns of local populations have contributed to these delays. These are urgent challenges to overcome. High cost must not serve as an excuse.

With approximately 40% of the United States' chemical weapon stocks destroyed, the US Government Accountability Office has reported that destruction would be completed in 2012 at the earliest. US delays are partly due to environmental and safety concerns.

The figures for Russia are even less satisfactory. Only approximately 4% of the Soviet Union's 40,000-tonne stockpile has been destroyed. Russia's destruction programme receives financial and technical assistance from the United States and the Cooperative Threat Reduction-type programmes of the European Union. Some causes of the delay have been the low levels of federal Russian funding, inefficient use of foreign assistance and persistent bureaucratic problems. However, during 2005 there were several positive developments in the Russian destruction programme. Still, notwithstanding Russia's improving economy and additional Russian resources combined with continued international assistance to Russia's destruction programme, it seems unlikely that the entire Russian chemical-weapon stockpile will be destroyed by 2012.

In addition to the destruction programmes in Russia and the United States, programmes to destroy chemical weapon stockpiles are also being carried out in Albania, India, Libya and South Korea, and efforts are ongoing to destroy the chemical weapons that Japan left in China after World War II.

WMDC RECOMMENDATION

37 States parties to the Chemical Weapons Convention must provide adequate resources to ensure that there are no undue delays in the agreed destruction of chemical weapon stockpiles.

Promoting universality

Sixteen states, as of April 2006, have not ratified the CWC, for a variety of reasons:

- Some may have chemical weapon programmes and may consider it not to be in their security interests to become a party.
- Some may not have chemical weapon programmes but may withhold participation for reasons of regional political leverage.
- Some have signalled an interest in joining the CWC but have not yet done so.
- Some may have no chemical industries and see no reason to join and finance the implementation of a treaty that does not directly affect them.

BOX 23

NON–PARTIES TO THE CWC, as of April 2006

States that have signed but not yet ratified:
Bahamas, Central African Republic, Comoros, Congo, Dominican Republic, Guinea-Bissau, Israel, Myanmar

Non-signatory states:
Angola, Barbados, Egypt, Iraq, Lebanon, North Korea, Somalia, Syria

The universal adherence of states to the CWC is important for the authority and effectiveness of the regime.

Both the OPCW and its individual member states may provide positive incentives to states still remaining outside the Convention to sign and ratify it. Some member states have also exerted political and economic pressure. For example, in accordance with the European Union WMD Strategy, in an agreement with Syria in October 2004, the EU insisted on Syria's taking steps towards adherence to the CWC as a precondition for entering into a bilateral Association Agreement.

WMDC RECOMMENDATION

38 The Organisation for the Prohibition of Chemical Weapons and states parties to the Chemical Weapons Convention should continue their efforts to secure universal adherence to the Convention. States parties should fully implement the rules on trade and transfer of chemicals that are precursors to chemical-weapon agents. They should further develop regulations regarding the trade and transfer of chemicals that can be used to produce chemical weapons. The Organisation for the Prohibition of Chemical Weapons and states parties should continue to offer states positive incentives, including technical assistance, to join and implement the Chemical Weapons Convention. When providing such assistance or transferring relevant technologies, they should consider steps to ensure safe and responsible handling by the recipient.

Non-lethal weapons, incapacitants and riot control agents

The term *non-lethal* weapons in the context of the CWC usually refers to riot control agents, such as tear gas and CS gas, and substances that can incapacitate by putting a person to sleep, often referred to as 'knock-out' gas. Yet the term non-lethal is misleading, since all of these gases can be lethal if the concentration is sufficiently high and the time of exposure sufficiently long. Similarly, substances that cause unconsciousness may be lethal in concentrations used to affect a large number of people simultaneously.

The use of riot control agents is specifically and explicitly prohibited in the CWC as a method of warfare. It may at first be difficult to understand why it is a violation of international law to use tear gas against combatants in war, but not necessarily a violation to use it against a civilian population in peacetime. The reason is that tear gas is used for riot control in peacetime to *avoid* the use of firearms, while riot control agents have a history of being used in wars to force combatants out of foxholes or bunkers to be exposed to lethal arms or explosives. Furthermore, any use of riot control agents risks provoking retaliation or an escalation in the choice of chemical agents.

States still say that they might need to use riot control agents for purposes other than warfare (e.g. a riot in a prison). International regulations relevant to such use are not laid down in the CWC but are found in the framework of human rights and international humanitarian law.

Increased interest in non-lethal chemical weapons

There is an increasing interest among some governments to adopt a more flexible interpretation of the CWC rules on the use of incapacitating chemical weapons, even as a method of warfare, in order to be able to use them in diverse situations.

Such an interpretation, in the view of the Commission, would constitute a dangerous erosion of the fundamental ban on chemical weapons that the authors of the Convention intended. If accepted, it might allow for use in armed conflict of substances such as fentanyl, a derivative of which was used in Moscow in 2002 when terrorists held hostages at a theatre and law enforcement units used the opiate to facilitate their attack. The opiate killed about one-fifth of the hostages. States parties and the OPCW should reaffirm that an interpretation of the CWC allowing the use of such substances in armed conflicts would not be consistent with the Convention.

The development of new non-lethal or less-than-lethal chemical weapons with incapacitating effects or other effects on the brain would, if accepted for use in armed conflicts, considerably change the nature of warfare and jeopardize the integrity of the CWC.

The general purpose criterion

The CWC provides means for protecting peaceful uses gained from technological advances, while maintaining and strengthening the barriers to hostile uses, through the *general purpose criterion* in Article 1 of the Convention.

Instead of prohibiting a particular chemical or family of chemicals, the CWC prohibits all toxic chemicals, except for 'the listed purposes'. These listed purposes include 'industrial, agricultural, research, medical, pharmaceutical or other peaceful purposes ... purposes directly related to protection against toxic chemicals ... military purposes not connected with the use of chemical weapons and not dependent upon the toxic properties of chemicals as a method of warfare; law enforcement including domestic riot control purposes'.

Toxic is defined in the CWC as anything that is harmful through 'chemical action on life processes', whether it is temporarily incapacitating or lethal. Some toxic substances that have been considered for use as disabling chemical weapons are even more toxic than the chemicals developed for lethal purposes, in the sense that extremely small amounts are sufficient to cause an effect.

The BTWC provides a similar general purpose criterion, prohibiting in Article I 'microbial or other biological agents, or toxins whatever their origin or method of production of types and in quantities that have no justification for prophylactic, protective or other peaceful purposes'. The inclusion not only of microbial agents, but also of toxins, captures such natural substances as those ligands and other naturally occurring bioactive molecules and their chemical analogues that can exert harmful effects on life processes. The CWC and the BTWC are therefore mutually reinforcing in their prohibition of toxicity as a weapon of war.

Provided the general purpose criterion is implemented properly, it ensures that the conventions remain relevant and effective even in the face of future technological advances in biochemistry and biotechnology. When new toxic chemicals are developed they automatically come under its purview. The Commission therefore holds that the prohibitions of the CWC cover all toxic chemicals, regardless of their origin or method of production, and that the general purpose criterion of the CWC is valid.

WMDC RECOMMENDATION

39 States parties to the Chemical Weapons Convention should confirm that, like the use of riot control agents, the use of toxic chemical agents for purposes of law enforcement is banned as a method
of warfare. Accordingly, each state party must declare any such
agent under Article III.

Enhancing the CWC's inspection and monitoring capacity

Pursuant to Article IX on consultations, cooperation and fact-finding, each party to the CWC has the right to request an *on-site challenge inspection* of any facility or location in any other state party, for the sole purpose of clarifying and resolving any questions concerning possible non-compliance with the Convention. The Commission underscores the importance of such inspections in strengthening the effectiveness and credibility of the CWC. The parties should not view challenge inspections solely as a means of last resort to clarify cases of suspected non-compliance. Rather, the parties should view such inspections as a confidence-building measure – a collective means to reinforce their commitment to the CWC.

For challenge inspections to be effective, the Technical Secretariat of the OPCW must have the necessary legal rights, resources and training as well as cooperation and assistance from states concerned. The OPCW requires up-to-date information from member states, and preferably the most up-to-date technical and inspection equipment. It further requires sampling rights and the ability to remove samples for testing, capabilities and permissions to facilitate rapid transport and entry to the requested location.

Not all states have provided such information or rights. In addition, the OPCW is currently limited to the use of an approved list of equipment agreed by states parties, and states may refuse to allow the use of some of the approved equipment. Inspected states must ensure that the most efficient equipment available shall be on the list of equipment agreed for use by the OPCW.

Training exercises for challenge inspections have been carried out in a few states, mainly in Europe. It would be valuable if more states and regions would conduct such exercises.

WMDC RECOMMENDATION

40 States parties should ensure that the Organisation for the Prohibition of Chemical Weapons has the resources, experience and legal rights needed to carry out challenge inspections in a timely and effective manner, including for the taking of samples and removal of samples for testing.

CHEMICAL TERRORISM

The threat that non-state actors might use chemical weapons became a reality when the Aum Shinrikyo Japanese sect used sarin in the 1994 Matsumoto attack and later in the attacks in the Tokyo subway in 1995.

Non-state actors such as terrorist groups have many options for targets and the time and manner of attack. However, there are significant technical difficulties associated with obtaining the necessary materials in sufficient quantities and purity. Transporting and effectively using chemical weapons against an intended target also pose difficulties.

For example, Aum Shinrikyo had access to ample financial resources, modern equipment and at least one laboratory where it could do research and arrange production over an extended period, as well as people with knowledge and skills. Yet the sect managed to produce only limited quantities of chemical agents, and these had high levels of impurity and were unsuitable for long-term storage. As a result, the attacks were less effective than they might have been. The case shows that it is difficult to produce and disperse these weapons in an efficient manner even where the basic capacities exist. The most potent weapons pose lethal threats also to the perpetrators themselves.

The threat of terrorist attacks against chemical industry

Rather than dispersing chemical weapons of their own, terrorists might attack plants or transport vessels containing hazardous chemicals and cause leakages or large releases of industrial chemicals.

The potential effects of an attack on a chemical plant (or trains of tank cars) are illustrated by some large industrial accidents such as that in Bhopal, India, when more than 3,000 people died after an accidental release of methylisocyanate from a pesticide plant in 1984. The accident in the same year at a liquefied gas storage facility in Mexico City, where explosions killed more than 500 and injured about 7,200 people, and the massive explosion at a fertilizer plant in Toulouse in 2001 are other examples. Such chemical industries exist in the vicinity of many cities and some are even located in cities. The regular transport of dangerous chemicals to and from such facilities also raises security risks.

How to reduce the danger

It is important that countries and governments ensure that they have effective national legal frameworks and capacities to control the relevant equipment, materials and expertise, as required by UN Security Council Resolution 1540.

Risks can be reduced through many different measures, some simple, some costly. For instance, chemical industries may be relocated away from urban areas to areas with little or no civilian population, transport may be routed away from concentrations of population, and hazardous materials may be distributed for storage in several sites.

Other measures that may and should be taken relate to increased physical security and the development of a *security culture*, in ways similar to those practised by the nuclear industry. However, the challenge is great, since the number of sensitive facilities that would need such improved protection is in the thousands, while in comparison there are rather few nuclear facilities.

Chemical industries must minimize the risk of insider threats and ensure that they possess the required skills and leadership to take necessary action and reduce damage if a leakage occurs.

The role of national governments and international cooperation

The role of national governments is to ensure through supervision, legislation or agreement that the industry has an adequate security culture and to provide for legal action against anyone who commits malicious acts at or against chemical sites.

Furthermore, there is a need to work towards common international standards of security for chemical facilities, to reduce the risk that terrorists will seek targets in a country where security is lagging.

WMDC RECOMMENDATION

41 Through their domestic laws and policies, all states should prohibit the production, possession and use of toxic chemicals and technologies for purposes that are banned by the Chemical Weapons Convention. States should ensure security in and for chemical facilities through legislation and agreement with industry. States should also develop national means to monitor that security standards are met.

WMDC RECOMMENDATION

42 States parties to the Chemical Weapons Convention should use the Organisation for the Prohibition of Chemical Weapons as a coordinating centre in the development of global standards for a chemical industry security culture. The Organisation should offer evaluation and security assistance at declared sites. States parties should also strengthen the capacity of the Organisation for the Prohibition of Chemical Weapons to provide practical assistance against chemical weapons, for instance detection equipment, alarm systems and medical antidotes.

Delivery means, missile defences, and weapons in space

CHAPTER 6

Delivery means, missile defences, and weapons in space

Earlier chapters in this report discuss the various types of WMD and the considerable differences among them in terms of their immediate and long-term effects, how they are produced and used, and the risks they pose both to their producers and to their victims. This chapter examines three subjects that are not exclusively related to any one of the categories of WMD – the means of delivery of WMD, the dangers of missile defences, and the risk of weaponization of outer space.

MEANS OF WMD DELIVERY

A simple device that is capable of producing mass destruction becomes a *weapon* only when its user is able to deliver such a device effectively to an intended target. This can occur in several ways. The first nuclear weapons were delivered by heavy, long-range bombers. As nuclear weapons became smaller and lighter over time, a wider variety of aircraft could also deliver them, including fighters, missiles and even unmanned aerial vehicles (UAVs). Other deployment options arose with the development of nuclear landmines, depth charges, artillery shells and air defence systems.

Chemical weapons have been delivered by bombs and artillery shells, but also simply by venting clouds of toxic gases over a target area, as occurred in World War I. Both biological and chemical agents can be delivered via aerosols into the air or directly into a water supply. Even fleas, ticks and rodents are possible means for disseminating highly infectious biological agents, as demonstrated by Japan during World War II.

In recent years, much of the national and international effort to control WMD delivery systems has focused on the dangers posed by ballistic and cruise missiles, because of their capabilities to deliver such weapons over considerable distances, with increasing accuracy, with little warning and without risk to pilots.

Missiles encompass a range of types and technologies, from ground-, sea- and air-launched cruise missiles to land- and sea-launched ballistic missiles, and they are often dual-use – that is, they can deliver conventional weapons or WMD, which greatly complicates their control. Because of the difficulty of achieving accurate missile flight paths, most long-range ballistic missiles that have been developed outside the technically advanced states are not considered suitable for the delivery of conventional warheads.

BOX 24

VARIOUS TYPES OF AERIAL DELIVERY SYSTEMS

Ballistic missile. A missile that is propelled by a rocket engine upon launch and coasts to its target on a ballistic path – like a tossed stone.

Cruise missile. A manoeuvrable missile propelled, usually at low altitudes, to its target by a jet engine that operates throughout the flight.

Manned aircraft.
Unmanned aerial vehicle (UAV). A pilotless aircraft.
Space-launch vehicle (SLV). A rocket intended to place a payload into space for peaceful purposes, although it can also be used to deliver a WMD.

All the countries that have pursued nuclear-weapon programmes have also pursued ballistic missile technologies, whether by importing or indigenously developing them. While not every country with a ballistic missile programme also seeks to acquire nuclear weapons, any state with a programme or an ambition to develop nuclear weapons will be likely to have a ballistic missile programme.

The development of ballistic missiles is, however, both technically demanding and expensive. Cruise missiles, other than the most technically advanced missiles, or UAVs may be more attractive than ballistic missiles owing to their lower cost ($50,000–200,000), ease of acquisition, and better accuracy and reliability. UAVs have a flight stability that may permit them to spray biological or chemical agents over a targeted area, and both their range and payload have been increasing in recent years and are likely to continue to do so.

Around 40 states are known to have acquired or developed ballistic missiles, but most have only short-range (<1,000 km) delivery capability. Fewer than a dozen states possess medium-range (1,000–1,300 km) missiles. In addition to the five NPT-defined nuclear-weapon states, India, Iran, Israel, Pakistan and North Korea also have such capabilities. Only the five NPT nuclear-weapon states have long-range (intercontinental) missiles.

Approaches for controlling missiles

Missiles as delivery vehicles for nuclear weapons were the main focus of the Cold War arms control treaties, including the SALT I and II agreements, the START I and II treaties, and the INF Treaty. Missiles are easier to count and destroy in a transparent fashion than are nuclear warheads; control of the missiles was therefore seen as an efficient way to limit the nuclear arms race. However, there are no adequate multilateral missile controls.

Since 1987, many states possessing or producing nuclear-capable missiles have joined the Missile Technology Control Regime (MTCR), an informal, voluntary, non-treaty-based arrangement, to coordinate their export controls of missiles and missile technology. The MTCR, currently with 34 participating states, has an agreed set of guidelines and an annex of controlled items. The guidelines contain standards for its participants to apply in their national export licensing decisions – the guidelines only address outright the export of missile production facilities. The scope of the regime has been expanded in recent years to encompass all missiles capable of delivering WMD – including UAVs, cruise missiles and space launch vehicles.

In November 2002, a group of states established the International Code of Conduct Against Ballistic Missile Proliferation, known as the Hague Code of Conduct (HCOC). Complementing the MTCR, the HCOC has a considerably larger membership (124 subscribing states as of April 2006) and is based on agreement on certain confidence-building measures, including pre-launch notifications and other transparency measures, while also discouraging the development, testing and deployment of such missiles.

The HCOC, however, has certain shortcomings, including the fact that states have not reported on their programmes. It could usefully be broadened to include cruise missiles and UAVs that are more suitable for the delivery of biological weapons and chemical weapons than ballistic missiles. The HCOC is an export control regime that is not legally binding, and it lacks a secretariat.

Two recent UN panels of government experts studying missiles in all their aspects have deliberated over the proliferation of ballistic and cruise missiles and technologies, and concluded that this presents serious concerns for international peace and security.[7] However, the panels could not agree on any recommendations, which indicates the sensitivities surrounding the possession of missiles, especially those regarded as strategically significant (whether for conventional or WMD warheads).

---

7. Report of the Secretary-General, 'The issue of missiles in all its aspects', A/57/229, 23 July 2002, and A/59/278, 18 August 2004.

A Russian proposal, a Global Control System (GCS) for the Non-Proliferation of Missiles and Missile Technologies, was discussed in 2000–2001, but it was not agreed or implemented. Its approach merits revisiting for purposes of arms control and non-proliferation. It consisted of four main components: transparency and confidence-building measures; security assurances; positive incentives (including low-cost launch services); and multilateral negotiations on further steps to control and prevent missile proliferation. As a first step, Russia proposed a multilateral transparency regime that would require prior notification for all missile launches and a joint data exchange centre (JDEC) to collect data on launches. Positive security guarantees for states that renounced national missile programmes were also proposed.

While the Preamble of the NPT cites a goal of eliminating both nuclear weapons 'and the means of their delivery', there is no multilateral treaty requiring missile disarmament. Initiatives in this field have instead focused on specific countries. The successful efforts to eliminate individual countries' arsenals of medium- and long-range ballistic missiles and their associated infrastructure (in Libya, Ukraine and South Africa) have shared certain characteristics. The missiles were eliminated as one part of a wider set of measures to facilitate integration of the countries into the international community. In Ukraine, external donors met a large share of the costs of missile destruction and rehabilitation of bases. In the case of Iraq, medium-range missile programmes were eliminated after the defeat of Iraq by a UN-authorized coalition.

WMDC RECOMMENDATION

43 MTCR member states should make new efforts to better implement and expand export controls on relevant materials and technology. States subscribing to the Hague Code of Conduct should extend its scope to include cruise missiles and unmanned aerial vehicles. They should establish a multilateral data exchange centre, based on the Russian-US initiatives for the exchange of data on missile launches from early-warning systems. Regional and international non-proliferation measures should include information exchanges, launch notification, and restrictions or bans on specific items or capabilities.

MISSILE DEFENCES

Developments in recent years have fuelled support in some countries for constructing defences against missiles. These developments include North Korea's flight test of a missile over Japan in 1998; the repeated conduct of missile tests in the Middle East (Iran and Israel) and in South Asia (Pakistan and India); and the continued development of missile systems by the NPT nuclear-weapon states. While proponents of missile 'shields' highlight the specific threats of WMD-capable missiles, there are inherent risks that construction of such systems could provoke a destabilizing offence-defence spiral with regard to missiles, missile defence and outer space.

For example, the deployment of missile defence systems by one state in a region could induce a regional rival to expand its missile arsenal or to develop missiles that are better able to penetrate the defence. The same basic logic sustained the ABM Treaty, which for many years prevented the Soviet Union (later Russia) and the United States from deploying strategic missile defence systems. Missile defence systems are also not entirely defensive in orientation – radars, surveillance systems, and even interceptors can also be used for offensive military purposes. Today, when states are seriously concerned about global terrorist threats, the expenditure of vast resources on missile defences has also been widely criticized as a waste of money, since terrorists have many ways of deploying WMD other than by missiles.

Other specific causes for concern include the June 2002 withdrawal from the ABM Treaty by the United States, its pursuit of a multi-layered ballistic missile defence system, and various research and development activities under way in the US and other states that may lead to the testing and deployment of weapons in space. Another cause of concern is that the Conference on Disarmament has for many years been unable to agree to commence negotiations on a treaty to prevent an arms race in outer space.

Illustrating the lack of an international consensus to move forward in addressing these threats, the report of the first UN panel on missiles noted that its participants held different views on 'the implications of missile defences for arms control and disarmament; the effects of missile defences as well as of missile defence cooperation on the further spread and refinement of missiles; the effects of missile defences on the weaponization of space; and the effects of missile defences in addressing growing vulnerabilities to missile threats and attacks.'[8]

----

8. A/57/229, paragraph 70, p. 19.

Several different missile defence architectures may be envisaged, with different implications. Smaller ('theatre') missile defence systems already exist, and further collaboration on such defences is envisaged, including Patriot, NATO's Medium Extended Air Defence and the surface-to-air medium-range air defence system. Ballistic missile defence systems are designed to detect attacking missiles; to track missiles and, where relevant, re-entry vehicles (warheads); to discriminate between warheads and decoys; and to destroy attacking missiles and/or warheads. Such requirements present particular technological, military and financial challenges and often call for systems with land, sea, air and space components.

Since its withdrawal from the ABM Treaty in 2002, the United States has undertaken the first land-based phase of its missile defence programme with the deployment of mid-course interceptors in Alaska and California. Two types of early (boost-phase) missile defence are also under consideration: sea-based and airborne lasers. The attraction of intercepting missiles in an early phase is that they then leave a clear signature of hot gases, and there is no problem in distinguishing between warhead and decoys or chaff. But there are also many disadvantages. In particular, in order to intercept a missile during a five- to eight-minute section of its flight, decision-making would probably need to be made automatic or delegated to the field, each option carrying a high risk of accidental or inadvertent launch of an interceptor.

Recent US defence budget requests have envisaged parallel paths to acquire both a ground-based and a space-based intercept capability. Described in various official US statements as the 'ultimate high ground', outer space is characterized as offering options not only for missile defence but also for a broad range of interrelated civil and military missions. The US Congress has been reluctant to allocate funding as requested and thus has slowed down developments, but this has not resulted in the abandonment of the objective of space-based interception. Concerns have continued to grow internationally that the US pursuit of ballistic missile defences is likely to increase nuclear dangers and reduce international security. The potential value of these systems is not in proportion to the risks they pose to the international community, including to the states possessing such systems.

WMDC RECOMMENDATION

44

States should not consider the deployment or further deployment of any kind of missile defence system without first attempting to negotiate the removal of missile threats. If such negotiations fail, deployments of such systems should be accompanied by cooperative development programmes and confidence-building measures to lower the risk of adverse effects on international peace and security, including the risk of creating or aggravating arms races.

THE WEAPONIZATION OF SPACE

The world now relies on space technology for security and other purposes, such as meteorology, environmental monitoring, disaster prevention, communications, education, entertainment and surveillance. Although outer space has not yet been specifically weaponized, it is already militarized, with a range of force-supporting technologies associated with what has been called the 'revolution in military affairs'. Space security approaches are further complicated because commercial systems may also have strategic, safety or arms control (monitoring, confidence-building and verification) value, and military uses are often combined with, or make use of, commercial space systems.

There are two broad categories of military assets: force-support assets (communications, command and control, sensor, target location and sur-

---

BOX 26

THREE TYPES OF WEAPONS FOR USE IN OR FROM SPACE

Space-strike weapons (which in the past included Soviet fractional orbital bombardment systems) may harness directed energy such as lasers, or rely on kinetic energy, in which the destructive force is supplied by the mass and velocity of projectiles. So-called kinetic kill weapons may also be armed with conventional explosives to increase their destructive power.

Anti-satellite (ASAT) weapons are intended to disable or destroy satellites.

Space-based ballistic missile defence (BMD) weapons – such as lasers, kinetic kill weapons and armed interceptors – would be intended to destroy ballistic missiles, in either their boost phase or mid-course flight trajectory.

veillance) and force-application assets, which in a space environment apply to: (1) space-strike weapons, (2) anti-satellite (ASAT) weapons, and (3) ballistic missile defence (BMD) weapons (see Box 26).

WMD-related dangers

The development of weapons designed to attack military satellites – which are used to monitor missile launches and compliance with arms control and disarmament treaties – poses grave dangers to international peace and security. Attacks on early-warning satellites could well be viewed as a prelude to a nuclear war. The acquisition by one state of such weapons would inspire others to follow suit, leading to a new arms race. Some states might again seek to develop a new generation of nuclear weapons for use in outer space.

The US space agency, NASA, has estimated that there are now in orbit about 11,000 objects of space debris larger than 10 cm.[9] Guidelines have been drafted for voluntary measures to mitigate space debris, intended for adoption by the UN Committee for the Peaceful Uses of Outer Space, but these have yet to be taken up, adopted or enforced. Concerns have grown in recent years that the research, development and deployment of weapons in space would substantially increase this debris, thereby creating new threats for both civilian and military surveillance and communications satellites. Experts continue to debate the scope and urgency of this challenge, however.

Current status of the outer space security regime

The stationing of nuclear weapons or any other WMD in outer space or placement of such weapons in orbit are both prohibited under the 1967 Outer Space Treaty (OST), but nuclear warheads on BMD interceptors launched from terrestrial bases are not prohibited, nor is the sub-orbital transit of outer space by nuclear warheads on ballistic missiles.

There are already a number of international treaties and instruments regulating space activities, but they do not cover the challenges posed by space-based weapons or BMD. In particular, although some agreements prohibit or restrict the deployment of weapons or use of force in outer space, the provisions are limited in scope and coverage. Moreover, none of the existing legal instruments unequivocally prevents the testing, deployment and use of weapons – other than nuclear, chemical and biological weapons – in outer space. As a step in the right direction, President Putin announced in the

---

9.   NASA, Orbital Degree Program Office, http://www.orbitaldebris.jsc.nasa.gov.

UN General Assembly on 25 September 2003 that Russia had assumed an 'obligation not to be the first to deploy offensive strike weapons in outer space'.

Although the major space-faring nations are parties to the OST, the treaty falls far short of universal membership (there are 98 parties as of April 2006). In 2007, the OST will be 40 years old. It is time for a review of this treaty. Because all states have a high stake in maintaining outer space as a secure environment for peaceful uses, even those states with little intention of developing their own military or space-launch capabilities should be encouraged to become parties to the OST. That would reinforce the regime and help to educate and involve all nations in protecting space as a shared resource for peaceful development and the enhancement of global security.

The Commission emphasizes that, given the dual-use nature of space activities, it is unfortunate that regulations dealing with the peaceful uses of outer space – including the activities of the UN General Assembly's Committee on the Peaceful Uses of Outer Space (COPUOS) – are separated from those that address military or weapons-related issues. The lack of an overall framework prevents the development of a coherent approach to future challenges to space security – for example, a code of conduct and collective approaches for debris mitigation or launch notification. Institutions for addressing the full range of space-related issues need to be overhauled and revitalized. Either the mandates of existing forums should be revised, or a new forum needs to be created to address space security in all its aspects.

WMDC RECOMMENDATION

45 All states should renounce the deployment of weapons in outer space. They should promote universal adherence to the Outer Space Treaty and expand its scope through a protocol to prohibit all weapons in space. Pending the conclusion of such a protocol, they should refrain from activities inconsistent with its aims, including any tests against space objects or targets on earth from a space platform. States should adapt the international regimes and institutions for space issues so that both military and civilian aspects can be dealt with in the same context. States should also set up a group of experts to develop options for monitoring and verifying various components of a space security regime and a code of conduct, designed *inter alia* to prohibit the testing or deployment of space weapons.

WMDC RECOMMENDATION

46 A Review Conference of the Outer Space Treaty to mark its 40th year in force should be held in 2007. It should address the need to strengthen the treaty and extend its scope. A Special Coordinator should be appointed to facilitate ratifications and liaise with non-parties about the reinforcement of the treaty-based space security regime.

Export controls, international assistance, and non-governmental actors

CHAPTER 7

Export controls, international assistance, and non-governmental actors

In this chapter, the Commission examines three areas relating to all types of WMD: improving transfer controls, increasing international assistance for non-proliferation and disarmament activities, and expanding public participation in efforts against WMD.

EXPORT CONTROLS AND OTHER CONTROLS ON THE MOVEMENT OF GOODS

States use export controls for many purposes, and controls related to WMD are no exception. They generate information needed by states to determine who is buying what, and thereby help a state to assess the risks associated with specific exports. Such assessments help governments prevent the export of items that would assist other states or groups to produce WMD or their delivery systems, and thereby help ensure compliance with legal non-proliferation obligations. Although export licences are processed before the shipment of goods, not at the border, other controls can also be implemented after exports occur. Through agreed visits or inspections, states can confirm the final uses of especially sensitive items, an increasingly important control given that many illicit transactions involve intermediaries – a problem epitomized by the intercontinental illicit nuclear supply network organized by Pakistani scientist A. Q. Khan.

These analytic and preventive functions of export controls make them a valuable part of the overall effort to combat WMD proliferation. In addition, the fact that export controls are applied to the business community provides one of the few linkages between the private sector and arms control. Efficient export control authorities have developed and implemented methods for conducting a systematic dialogue with industry that involves a useful exchange of information for combating proliferation.

In the 1990s, groups of major states with capabilities to export WMD-related commodities expanded their joint efforts to develop or revitalize uniform export control standards, particularly for dual-use goods – items that can be used for either military or civilian purposes. More states now (as of April 2006) participate in the activities of the main multilateral arrangements: the Australia Group (39 states plus the European Commission), the Missile Technology Control Regime (34), the Nuclear Suppliers Group (45), the Zangger Committee (35) and the Wassenaar Arrangement on Export Controls for Conventional Arms and Dual-Use Goods and Technologies (40) – and participation continues to grow.

Over the years, however, the limited membership of these arrangements has served to erode both their legitimacy and their effectiveness. Critics have long maintained that these groups are exclusive clubs or cartels that have no right to try to dictate global standards for the rest of the world. Limited membership arrangements also suffer from the fact that a growing number of producers of sensitive commodities are not members, which increases the risk that illicit importers will simply choose to do business with suppliers who offer items with the fewest controls.

There is also a need to strengthen the informal communications from the export control arrangements to the IAEA and the OPCW, to assist these organizations in their verification tasks.

UN Security Council Resolution 1540 requires all states to put in place appropriate effective national export and trans-shipment controls on nuclear, chemical and biological weapons, their means of delivery and related materials. These controls must be law-based and must be sufficient to control export, transit, trans-shipment and re-export. The resolution requires states to establish and enforce appropriate criminal or civil penalties for violations of such laws and regulations. The implementation of Resolution 1540 must be sensitive to current proliferation threats and to the need to facilitate, rather than obstruct, legitimate trade.

Changes in the international marketplace, and in the way in which technology transfer takes place, have challenged traditional export controls. The availability of a much wider class of dual-use items and technologies has required a growing use of end-use controls. In addition, global industrial cooperation involving such items has created a need for effective controls on intangible technology transfers that do not involve physical items. The existence of clandestine purchasing networks, and the potential insider threats at specialized companies and research centres, will also require governments to maintain controls over intra-state commerce involving WMD-related goods.

Taken together, these developments suggest the need for a broader perspective on how to move from a system of control based on barriers to exports to one that addresses all aspects of the potentially dangerous ownership and circulation (both within and between states) of WMD-related goods, and that does so in a more inclusive and cooperative way than before. This would be grounded in permanent cooperation with the business sector. It would require proliferation-sensitive transactions to be assessed against universally agreed criteria, regardless of the location of the end-user. Consultations to devise options for such a system could start at an informal expert level, with representatives from government, international organizations and industry. Initially, a suitable framework could be regional economic bodies, such as the European Union, which already have mechanisms for liaison and dialogue with industry.

Control of movement of goods

The difficulties of preventing proliferation-related activities hiding under the cover of legitimate commerce led the United States in May 2003 to launch the Proliferation Security Initiative (PSI), which focuses on interdicting and seizing illicit shipments while in transit. By September 2003, the United States had assembled a coalition consisting of 10 additional states (Australia, France, Germany, Italy, Japan, the Netherlands, Poland, Portugal, Spain and the United Kingdom), which agreed to a Statement of Interdiction Principles. Since then, many additional countries have joined this initiative, including all members of the EU and the G8.

Described by one of its architects as an 'activity' rather than a 'treaty-based bureaucracy', the PSI has encouraged greater international cooperation in undertaking interdictions, including joint participation in a number of exercises organized in different regions. Its participants have stressed that the interdiction activities will be undertaken in a manner that is consistent with international law.

It is difficult, however, and perhaps somewhat premature to assess the value of the PSI, as little concrete information has so far been made available to the public about its application, beyond press releases about interdiction exercises and official claims that it has been a great success. Although the initiative has gained the support of a large number of states, it has also generated concerns among critics who prefer a more multilateral approach, tied more closely to the treaty regimes and the UN Security Council.

The launch of the PSI marks the first time that states and organizations have cooperated to improve the security of the full supply chain for goods in international trade. Efforts have also been made in recent years to control the movement of thousands of large shipping containers that travel through world commerce each day. Such efforts have led to new capacities and cooperation for outbound inspection (for export control enforcement), and inbound inspection (for threat reduction), and control of goods and individuals at borders. Technology is being sought to make this process as nonintrusive as possible. The World Customs Organization (WCO) is also working to secure and protect the international trade supply chain from being used for acts of terrorism or other criminal activity.

WMDC RECOMMENDATION

47 All states should conduct audits of their export control enforcement agencies (customs, police, coastguard, border control and military) to ensure that they can carry out their tasks effectively. States should seek to establish a universal system of export controls providing harmonized standards, enhanced transparency and practical support for implementation. Members of the five export control regimes should promote a widening of their membership and improve implementation in view of current security challenges, without impeding legitimate trade and economic development.

INTERNATIONAL ASSISTANCE FOR NON-PROLIFERATION AND DISARMAMENT

Since the early 1990s, there has been a rapid growth of practical measures to facilitate disarmament, non-proliferation and counter-terrorism. Such measures are often jointly implemented in one state with several cooperating parties, including other states, international organizations, local and regional governments, non-governmental organizations (NGOs) and the private sector. The most ambitious programme of this kind is the Global Partnership Against the Spread of Weapons and Materials of Mass Destruction agreed by the Heads of State and Government of the G8 countries meeting in Kananaskis, Canada, in June 2002.

There are three types of measures for international non-proliferation and disarmament assistance (INDA): facilitating the dismantlement and destruction of weapons; establishing a chain of custody over weapons or weapons-usable materials; and demilitarization projects.

Activities have included the provision of technical assistance, training, equipment and financing. The aim of INDA may include not only withholding dangerous materials from terrorists and proliferators, but also other military and non-military security objectives, including environmental protection and nuclear safety. INDA helps to build confidence and solidarity between states and to bind them into a cooperative security relationship. Russia has so far received the lion's share of INDA and is likely to do so in the foreseeable future.

One project that should be actively pursued is the Elimination of Weapons-Grade Plutonium Production (EWGPP) programme. This programme seeks to close down the last remaining reactors in Russia that were originally built to supply plutonium for nuclear weapons but that also provide cities with electricity. Upon shutdown, the reactors will be monitored under the US-Russian Plutonium Production Reactor Agreement (PPRA).

Completing the EWGPP programme would contribute to two key objectives. First, destroying facilities that were created to produce plutonium for nuclear weapons would offer a rare case of a nuclear-weapon state reducing its military nuclear establishment in an irreversible way.[10] Second, the EWGPP programme and the PPRA monitoring system will be important contributions to developing verifiable assurances that nuclear-weapon states are no longer producing fissile material for military purposes. This would strongly support the development of a fissile material cut-off treaty, while at the same time preventing production of substantial amounts of weapons-grade plutonium.

In the biological field, INDA offers opportunities for cooperation to reduce dangers arising from past programmes, as well as current and future development of facilities. Biosecurity projects should be developed and financed under the Global Partnership. All countries with facilities working with dangerous pathogens or toxins should be eligible for financial support.

There is potential for the INDA approach in countries other than Russia. In particular, measures to assure the chain of custody over sensitive materials and to prevent misapplication of scientific and engineering skills have wider relevance. In states that have abandoned their WMD programmes, increased transparency and international participation in the demilitarization process have advanced the security interests of these states and their wider neighbourhoods.

---

10. France has also shut down and is dismantling its military plutonium production facilities.

WMDC RECOMMENDATION

48 The G8 Global Partnership should expand the geographical and functional scope of its non-proliferation assistance. The G8 should guarantee full funding for the Elimination of Weapons-Grade Plutonium Production (EWGPP) programme. Potential donors should consider how technical assistance, training, equipment and financing could be brought to bear to help states of all regions implement UN Security Council Resolution 1540.

SECTORAL ROLES: BUSINESS, RESEARCH, VOLUNTARY ORGANIZATIONS AND THE PUBLIC

National decisions on WMD should be transparent and democratic, and should not be monopolized by the 'security priesthoods'. Those seeking to eliminate such weapons have particularly good reasons to try to get non-governmental constituencies involved, since public pressure has often been exercised in favour of arms control and restraint.

However, there are also practical reasons to review the potential of cross-sectoral (state, corporate and popular) interaction on this subject. At some point, taxpayers have paid for all the WMD objects in existence, and they will also pay for the efforts to safely dispose of them.

This section addresses specific aspects of corporate, civil and individual roles in reaction to WMD that are not dealt with elsewhere in the report.

The responsibility of companies and the business sector

Private business needs to participate in developing and implementing responsible controls that extend to exports of both tangible and intangible goods. No legitimate company wants to have the reputation of being an illicit supplier of WMD goods and technology. This applies not only to producers, but also to other members of the business community, including shippers, insurers, bankers, freight forwarders, marketing specialists, business lawyers and many other related professions. Their support needs to be mobilized in the same transnational dimension in which the illicit trade takes place.

Governments and international organizations with competence in the security or trade/industrial fields should organize dialogues with the corresponding business sectors. Such interaction is needed to ensure that businesses are informed about, supported in implementing and invited to help in defining the obligations that apply to them in respect of WMD-related technology control. This pertains to dual-use technology, safety regulations, anti-terrorism measures, transport security and other relevant spheres. WMD-relevant businesses should also be encouraged to network – nationally, regionally and sectorally – to help each other raise standards and to establish best-practice norms for their sectors, in keeping with *inter alia* UN Security Council Resolution 1540.

WMDC RECOMMENDATION

49 Companies engaged in activities relevant to weapons of mass destruction have the ability and responsibility to help prevent the proliferation of such weapons and an interest in demonstrating that they are fulfilling that responsibility, including full compliance with national and international obligations and public transparency. Trade associations should promote such objectives.

The responsibility of scientists: codes of conduct

Codes of conduct and practice for scientists can have an important impact on how present and future threats from WMD-related materials, technology and know-how are handled. Such codes offer a means to address the dual-use problem, particularly in the biological field, given scientific and technological advances and persisting concerns that bio-defence work could serve as a cover for a clandestine biological weapon programme.

Particularly essential is an increased personal awareness of how research could be misused, and a culture of integrity and responsibility fostered through scientific oversight, peer review, pre-publication review and 'whistle blowing' mechanisms. Consideration and discussion of ethical questions should help scientists establish when a given activity might not be compatible with a state's international legal commitments and should therefore be suspended, slowed or otherwise modified pending the results of a final evaluation.

Codes of conduct are needed to give guidance to scientists whose expertise could be used to support WMD-related activities. Both national and international forums have a role to play in preparing, evaluating and reviewing the implementation of such codes, a matter under consideration in parallel processes under the auspices of the International Committee of the Red Cross and UNESCO. Work is currently being carried out at the international level by, for example, the states parties to the BTWC and the International Union of Pure and Applied Chemistry (IUPAC).

Codes of practice for individuals could also usefully be developed by industry. These could be modelled on the biosafety controls used by the pharmaceutical industry, known as 'good manufacturing practice"' and 'good microbiological technique'.

WMDC RECOMMENDATION

50 States, international organizations and professional associations should encourage the appropriate academic and industrial associations to adopt and effectively implement codes of practice and codes of conduct for science and research in weapons of mass destruction-relevant fields.

Democratic control: role of representative institutions

Nations possessing nuclear weapons, and those in the process of disposing of CW and BW materials, vary greatly in how openly they define and debate their corresponding policies; how specifically they identify the national resources devoted to WMD production, purchase, operation and disposal; and what, if any, roles they allow their parliamentary institutions to play in these matters.

Such institutions should receive and debate information on WMD holdings, their cost and the policy purposes they are deemed to serve. Applying higher and more consistent standards in this respect would not only foster greater responsibility, accountability and answerability on the part of governments, but also reinforce the message that it is governments rather than the military that decide in these matters. Interparliamentary cooperation and exchange of information and visits should be encouraged.

WMDC RECOMMENDATION

51 Governments possessing any weapons of mass destruction should keep their parliaments fully and currently informed of their holdings of such weapons and their activities to reduce and eliminate them. Parliaments should actively seek such information and recognize their responsibility in formulating policies relevant to weapons of mass destruction issues. Greater inter-parliamentary cooperation on weapons of mass destruction issues is needed.

Democratic control: NGOs and transparency

The activities of non-governmental organizations have been the main chan-
nel for conveying views and proposals about WMD from the grass roots to
governments and international organizations. They have at times exercised
a tangible influence on official decisions in the direction of eliminating WMD,
while also preventing new acquisitions, technical development, and additional deployments and testing.

In particular, women's organizations have often played a vital role – from
the Hague peace conferences of the 19th century to the present time. The role
of women in the maintenance and promotion of peace and security was recognized by the Security Council in Resolution 1325 (2000). Women have rightly
observed that armament policies and the use of armed force have often been
influenced by misguided ideas about masculinity and strength. An understanding of and emancipation from this traditional perspective might
help to remove some of the hurdles on the road to disarmament and non-
proliferation.

NGOs' own choices determine how much pressure they will exert on
WMD issues in proportion to, say, landmines or other issues at any given
time. NGOs have for obvious reasons been more active on the WMD front in
states with democratic political systems. Open societies also make it easier
for NGOs to address and ally with other actors, such as political parties,
parliament, the media, trade unions and responsible businesses.

Obstacles that are beyond the control of NGOs include the reluctance of
some governments to permit them to pursue anti-WMD campaigns (normally on grounds of national security); the reluctance of other governments
and institutions to listen to and be influenced by them; the lack of reliable and
comparable data on the problem; and the lack of financial support.

By definition, the NGO role should not be the subject of any official edict
or set framework. The Commission hopes that its report will inspire NGOs
all over the world to renew their demands for transparency, free debate on
WMD and the eventual elimination of all related threats.

WMDC RECOMMENDATION

52 States should assist Non-Governmental Organizations to actively participate in international meetings and conferences, and to inform and campaign in the weapons of mass destruction field. Private foundations should substantially increase their support for such organizations that are working to eliminate global weapons of mass destruction threats.

Public information and education

Without adequate knowledge or concern at the popular level, neither parliaments nor NGOs can be expected to exercise effective pressure on governments regarding WMD issues, nor are businesses likely to feel pressure to play their own responsible roles. In fact, manifestations of public concern about WMD have varied widely over both time and place, as a function of access to information and the public's own attitudes and priorities. In the Euro-Atlantic region, while general levels of concern about WMD remain high, especially with regard to terrorist threats, this concern has not inspired a new wave of political demands for nuclear disarmament. This is likely due to the decline in public fears of the risk of strategic nuclear attacks in the Post-Cold War era. Yet interest in disarmament is still strong in locations where such weapons have been used, as illustrated by the network of mayors addressing nuclear threats.[11]

The shifting both of actual threats and of fashions in thinking about them has repeatedly re-directed attention – towards safety risks from the civil rather than military use of the nuclear sector; towards risks of WMD proliferation rather than possession; towards the threat from terrorists rather than states; towards low-tech weapons like landmines and small arms rather than hi-tech ones; and away from armaments-related issues altogether. Against this background it is easy to see why WMD disarmament continues to remain low on many people's list of priorities, both inside and outside of government.

In 2001–2002 an international panel of experts prepared a report for the United Nations on 'Disarmament and Non-Proliferation Education'. It was presented in the General Assembly's First Committee in October 2002. The

---

11. The mayors of Hiroshima and Nagasaki have organized an international 'Mayors for Peace' initiative to promote nuclear disarmament. As of March 2006, its membership stood at 1,306 cities in 115 countries and regions (www.mayorsforpeace.org).

United Nations General Assembly has since then adopted two resolutions that have 'conveyed' the recommendations of this study to all UN member states.[12] The report highlighted the changing context of arms-related threats and remedies and pointed out that a range of different methods were needed to raise the level of public consciousness, understanding, and engagement in different age groups and different sectors of society. It stressed the need for materials in many languages and for full exploitation of modern electronic media; and called for partnership with all interested institutions and NGOs inside and outside the UN system. Although it was largely uncontentious, follow-up on the report has been gradual and incomplete.

WMDC RECOMMENDATION

53 Organizations with security-relevant agendas should re-examine the 2002 United Nations Study on Disarmament and Non-Proliferation Education, and should consider ways in which they could foster and support such education and an informed public debate. Governments should fund student internships at multilateral institutions working on weapons of mass destruction issues.

---

12. A/RES/57/60, 30 December 2002 and A/RES/59/93, 16 December 2004.

Compliance, verification, enforcement and the role of the United Nations

CHAPTER 8

Compliance, verification, enforcement and the role of the United Nations

Before the 1991 Gulf War, efforts to rid the world of weapons of mass destruction were directed mainly at getting states to commit themselves to arms control and disarmament treaties and to agree on new ones. The 1972 Biological and Toxin Weapons Convention built on the rules of the 1925 Geneva Protocol prohibiting the use of chemical and bacteriological weapons. The rules of the Protocol were further developed and strengthened in the 1993 Chemical Weapons Convention.

Many treaty-based restrictions on nuclear weapons seemed to function well, such as those embodied in the 1963 Partial Test-Ban Treaty and the prohibitions on the stationing of nuclear weapons in the 1959 Antarctic Treaty, the 1967 Outer Space Treaty, the 1971 Seabed Treaty and various regional agreements establishing nuclear-weapon-free zones. The intention, still unfulfilled, was to supplement them by treaties that comprehensively prohibited the testing of nuclear weapons and the production of fissile material for weapon purposes.

While issues relating to implementation – monitoring and verification, compliance, and enforcement – were certainly recognized as significant, they were generally not in the forefront. In the effort to prevent nuclear-weapon proliferation, many thought, not unreasonably, that it was more important to focus on countries that refused to join the NPT than on weaknesses in the safeguards system. If a country wanted to develop nuclear weapons, so it was reasoned, it would refrain from adhering to the NPT rather than joining the treaty and violating it. At the time, India, Pakistan, Israel, South Africa, Argentina and Brazil were all outside the treaty.

Even though the world condemned the violations of the Geneva Protocol committed during the war between Iraq and Iran in 1980–1988, these violations did not become a major international issue, as they should have.

After the 1991 Gulf War and the revelation of Iraq's WMD programmes, greater attention was given to the brutal and illegal use of chemical weapons and the violations of the NPT and the BTWC. Not long after these revelations, the IAEA concluded in 1993 that North Korea had violated its safe-guards agreement with the Agency. There was a strong suspicion that North Korea might be engaged in a nuclear weapon programme. Not surprisingly, questions were raised whether the increasing number of parties to the NPT might be accompanied by more non-compliance. Were treaty commitments merely lulling the law-abiding states into a false and dangerous confidence? How effective was international verification? Can treaties on arms control and disarmament be enforced? How and by whom?

This chapter focuses on the role of treaties and on compliance, verification and enforcement. In the last section, it discusses the UN institutions that are needed for the negotiation and implementation of treaties and other norms of arms control and disarmament.

Treaties as tools to restrict or ban WMD

Governments know that treaties are indispensable. They see many multilateral treaties as an essential part of a commonly agreed and commonly managed world order, which most want to strengthen. The Commission supports that view.

There are good reasons, especially where universal adherence to common norms is sought – as in the sphere of arms control and disarmament – why states define required future conduct in treaties:

- Multilateral treaties have emerged over a long period of time as the principal instrument that the world community uses to create clear rules and standards designed to bind all states.
- Participation in the negotiation of a treaty of universal reach, or joining such a treaty, allows a state to feel ownership of and responsibility for the rules that are adopted.
- The formal and sometimes solemn procedures for adherence to a treaty serve to increase the credibility of a state's commitment to conduct itself in conformity with rules that have been agreed.
- The procedure of national consent may involve both the executive and the legislative branches of a government, thereby anchoring the international rules more firmly in the national consciousness.
- Rights and obligations are defined by the treaty. A measure of stability is created when states parties are able to predict that other parties are likely to conduct themselves in accordance with the obligations they have assumed. At the same time there is some protection against arbitrary demands and accusations.

■ The treaty may offer a basis for monitoring, verification, inspection, resolution of disputes or other action, such as periodic review and follow-up.

COMPLIANCE

Treaty obligations are generally respected for a number of very good reasons:

First, they lay down rules that have been expressly accepted by the parties. In the cases of the multilateral BWTC, CWC and NPT, a vast number of states parties share the view that such weapons are abhorrent; they see no need or use for them and want them to be outlawed. By adhering to such treaties, many states may also want to join the mainstream and help gradually build up a world order that, while demanding restraints for themselves, also gives them a fairly high assurance that others will exercise the same restraints.

Second, the global arms control treaties – those open to all states of the world – have been negotiated in ways that have taken into account many specific national concerns. Concessions have been made mutually.

Third, just as citizens for the most part respect the law not out of fear of punishment or other consequences for violations but because they accept the need for law and want to be seen as law-abiding, governments habitually respect their treaty commitments because they want to be respectable members of the international community. Treaty obligations are legal thresholds. The cost for a government to be seen as an unreliable treaty partner could be very high. The rapid and accelerating pace of international integration makes all states, even the biggest and strongest, ever more dependent upon one another.

Fourth, apart from the general benefit of global respect for desired norms, adherence to and compliance with treaties may bring specific rewards, such as a facilitated transfer of technology and technical assistance. Conversely, non-compliance with a treaty is likely to be discouraged by the risk of economic or other pressures, possibly sanctions, brought by the international community or individual states.

Nevertheless, non-compliance with treaty obligations, including those under arms control agreements, might well meet only oral condemnation, especially if the guilty party is a big and strong state or invulnerable for some other reason. Yet, just as national laws are rarely discarded because of violations, treaties are also rarely abandoned because of a few violations.

The reasons for compliance can hardly justify a downgrading of treaties as crucial instruments for achieving desirable common, predictable and mostly reliable conduct by states. Until the international community develops more effective systems to create and uphold common rules, the world has to make do with an ever-expanding fabric of treaties that regulate trade, communications, human rights, arms control and disarmament and that create institutions which play a role in the administration of the rules.

VERIFICATION

One state's non-compliance with its obligations under a treaty on arms control or disarmament may fundamentally and negatively affect the security of others. A bilateral treaty may simply be abrogated. In a global context, this may lead to collective reactions. Conversely, continued compliance with such treaty obligations impacts positively on security. In both cases, credible verification to establish compliance or non-compliance is of major importance.

There is no doubt that verification carried out on behalf of the international community through its various institutions deserves and enjoys much more credibility than verification carried out by the organs of individual states. Verification provides in itself an inducement to compliance, as detection of non-compliance is likely to have negative consequences.

Verification of compliance may be simple or difficult. A violation of the Partial Test-Ban Treaty (PTBT) through a nuclear test in the atmosphere would be detected quickly. Laboratory research on a virus for use in biological weapons might be hard to discover.

The readiness among states to accept verification, particularly on-site inspection, has developed gradually. Under the Geneva Protocol of 1925, states are prohibited from using chemical and bacteriological weapons. When this agreement was negotiated, there would have been strong resistance to any obligatory mechanisms or procedures for verification, and none was established. It was assumed that any violation would be manifest.

During the Cold War, the Soviet Union was a rigidly closed empire that would not accept any meaningful on-site inspections. The PTBT was accepted without any special mechanism for inspection, as tests in the atmosphere could be easily detected throughout the world. In the same period, important national technical means of detection were developed. Overhead surveillance was made technically possible through high-altitude flights (by U2 planes) and, later, satellite imagery from international space. Such national technical means are still used extensively by a number of states. They are supplemented by many advanced modern techniques, for example, electronic eavesdropping, and the age-old method of espionage. A political break-through for aerial surveillance in the Euro-Atlantic area is the 2002 Treaty on Open Skies that establishes a regime of observation flights to gather information about military forces and activities of the 30 states parties, from Vancouver to Vladivostok.

Verification through on-site inspection

With the expanded use of nuclear energy and the adoption of the NPT in 1968, international inspection became necessary. The NPT non-nuclear-weapon states began to enter into safeguards agreements with the IAEA and to declare all their fissile material open to inspections. The inspectors had professional nuclear experience and were employed as international civil servants.

Much more intrusive inspections were mandated by the Security Council for Iraq after the Gulf War (especially by Resolution 687 of 1991). In the biological, chemical and missile fields these inspections were carried out by UNSCOM and later by UNMOVIC. In the nuclear area, the IAEA was responsible.

The 1993 Chemical Weapons Convention established an elaborate system of verification that was modeled on the IAEA safeguards system, but in several respects it was more advanced. No system of verification has yet been developed to verify compliance with the Biological Weapons Convention, which was concluded at a time (1972) when general acceptance of effective on-site inspection would have been impossible.

The main function of the IAEA safeguards system under the NPT was to verify that nuclear material in non-nuclear-weapon states would not be diverted to weapons or for purposes unknown, and thus to create confidence that states parties complied with their obligations not to acquire nuclear weapons. A second aim was to provide timely detection of any diversion of a significant quantity of enriched uranium or plutonium, allowing other states and the international community time to take diplomatic or other action. A third aim was that the risk of detection should serve to deter state parties from violating their obligations. Verification was thus thought to have a direct bearing on compliance.

The IAEA safeguards arrangements, which are less than 50 years old, were the world's first global on-site inspection system. Not surprisingly, the reluctance of governments to accept highly intrusive international inspection at the time led to some serious weaknesses in the system. These made it easier for Iraq, Libya and Iran to violate their safeguards commitments without initially being detected. The non-compliance by Iraq that was discovered through the Gulf War convinced governments that the IAEA safeguards system had to be strengthened. This was done through the adoption of the Additional Protocol in 1997.

What inspection powers are appropriate?

The answer to this question depends on the level of ambition being sought. It is impossible to aim for complete assurance of a total absence of prohibited items or activities. Moreover, a hypersensitive system would be very costly and would result in many false and potentially troublesome alarms. In Japan and the United States, national police authorities, with all their resources and rights of access, failed to suspect and detect the illegal presence of sarin and anthrax that came to be used by non-state actors (in 1995 and 2001).

The strengthened safeguards system adopted and endorsed by the IAEA in 1997 probably marks the maximum that states are ready to accept today. It provides significant new powers for the inspectors and uses significant new techniques. It might not catch a non-compliant state red-handed. Rather than allowing this to happen, a non-compliant state will probably deny inspectors access to evidence – to a site, document or piece of equipment. Nevertheless, fire may not be needed as an alarm. Smoke may be enough.

As of March 2006, 75 states have accepted the strengthened IAEA safeguards system. It is vital for confidence that NPT non-nuclear-weapon states accept them as standard. It would be reasonable to make such safeguards a condition for the export of any nuclear items.

It has been suggested that evidence of a strategic authoritative decision by a government to comply with a specific commitment, rather than evidence from on-site inspections, should be the decisive test of compliance. While in the case of South Africa there was evidence of such a decision in its conduct, this was not sufficient to be the conclusive test. There had to be extensive inspection as well. In the case of Iraq, a 'strategic decision' had actually been taken, but the conduct of Iraq pointed in the opposite direction.

Thorough on-site inspection by competent international inspectors and the acquisition of objective data must provide the main basis for the international community's judgement of compliance. This will require extensive rights of access to sites, people and documents.

Governments can assist independent international inspections by supplying relevant information obtained through their national means of intelligence. They can also exert pressure and threaten sanctions to ensure that adequate access to sites and persons is given. The support given by the UN Security Council and its individual members to the inspections in Iraq was of crucial importance for their effective pursuit.

The Special Committee on Safeguards and Verification, which was established by the Board of Governors of the IAEA in 2005 and which may meet at any time, could play a useful role. Inspected states will be aware that resistance to or obstruction of inspections might meet with serious questioning not only from the international secretariat but also from many interested states. However, members of the committee must take care not to undermine the authority given to the international secretariat and to politicize what should remain objective technical investigations.

The inspection process

The technical means and processes used by inspectors have improved with some 50 years of experience. The inspections in Iraq stimulated the introduction of new, powerful methods such as environmental sampling and ground-penetrating radar. Similarly, aerial surveillance and photography have developed rapidly. New technical means allow inspection authorities to carry out continuous surveillance of sensitive installations and activities and to be informed directly and in real time. Such surveillance may both be cost-effective and help to avoid frequent intrusive visits by inspectors to equipment or sites. However, it will not obviate the need for periodic and unannounced visits on the ground by well-trained inspectors.

Theoretically, there would be nothing to prevent the UN Security Council from asking an individual member government to set up inspection teams from its own cadres for a particular inspection task. However, the nature of the task, which is one of objective fact-finding, will generally demand inspection teams that are independent of individual governments. Inspectors should be international civil servants who are not allowed to take instructions from or act on behalf of any individual government. The political organs to which inspectors report should be able to expect unbiased reports as the basis for their deliberations and decisions.

A good deal of experience has been accumulated about cooperation between international inspection authorities and national intelligence agencies, especially in the case of Iraq. National intelligence agencies may acquire information through such means as electronic and aerial surveillance, export controls and intelligence gathering. Their need to protect sources and techniques sets limits on the information they can provide to international inspectors. Nevertheless, it is clear that national intelligence services can greatly assist international inspection by providing important information – as they did in the case of Iraq and perhaps other cases. However, it is crucial that this remain a one-way street. Inspectors and inspections must not become the extended arms of intelligence services – otherwise, as experience has shown, they will lose their credibility and international respect.

WMDC RECOMMENDATION

54 As the strengthened safeguards system adopted by the International Atomic Energy Agency through the Additional Protocol should become standard for parties to the Non-Proliferation Treaty, supplier states should make acceptance of this standard by recipient parties a condition for contracts involving nuclear items.

WMDC RECOMMENDATION

55 Governments should instruct their intelligence authorities to assist international inspection agencies by providing relevant information without compromising the independence of the inspection systems.

Limitations on what can be achieved

First, proving the negative is rarely possible. It is sometimes demanded that inspections should result in 'clean bills of health' – full confidence about full compliance. This is hardly attainable. However, a high degree of thoroughness in inspection makes it likely that when no irregularities are found it is because there are none. The professionalism of the inspectors, the powers, the tools and the time given to them all matter. There will normally remain a residue of uncertainty that must be indicated in the reports. Determining how large a residue is tolerable is the responsibility of the political institutions to which the reports are submitted.

Second, the inspection organizations are not international police forces that can arrest and stop wrongdoers. However, they constitute important, impartial search machines with a degree of legal access that is unlikely to be given to foreign states. Although their vision is not unlimited, what they see and report is a vital contribution to the knowledge on which governments and the international community must base their conclusions and actions.

Third, the extensive discussions about the grounds on which some governments launched the war in Iraq indicate that these governments attributed little, if any, importance to the cautious and critical assessments presented as a result of the international inspections on the ground in Iraq. They chose instead to base their decisions on evidence that was presented to them by their own intelligence agencies, which turned out to be largely erroneous. The conclusion that should be drawn is that just as international inspection may benefit from information provided from national intelligence, which relies on a host of sources unavailable to international organizations, national governments would benefit from paying attention to what independent international inspection reports and recommends on the basis of on-site inspections and detached, professional analysis.

Is there a need for an inspection unit attached to the UN Security Council?

Currently, international verification of compliance with global bans on chemical weapons and nuclear proliferation is compartmentalized. In addition, verification of compliance is not provided for in the treaty banning biological weapons. Against this background, and given the relatively recent engagement shown by the UN Security Council in the threats related to WMD, it is not surprising that there have been suggestions for creating a permanent inspection unit as a subsidiary organ to the Security Council. However, it would hardly be practical to create parallel inspection functions that are already entrusted to (or may be conferred upon) the independent organizations that report to the UN – the IAEA and the OPCW.

The above conclusion in no way negates the idea of a technical unit attached to the Security Council. Such a unit could have a small core staff of professional inspectors who provide the Council with analyses, surveys and advice of a technical character. It should be able, when so requested by the Council, to set up and direct ad hoc inspection teams recruited from a roster of experts whom the unit keeps trained and up-to-date on the latest techniques. It should be based in and work with the UN Secretariat. As experience has shown in the case of inspections in Iraq, such a unit would gain in effectiveness if it were formally constituted as a subsidiary body of the Security Council.

There is currently no capacity to conduct inspections or monitoring that the Security Council might mandate in the fields of biological weapons and missiles. One possibility would be to convert the capability of the UN's Iraq inspection unit (UNMOVIC) into a unit for use by the Council or by the Secretary-General. For example, in a settlement of the current controversy regarding North Korea, effective verification of a ban on the acquisition or development of any weapons of mass destruction on the whole Korean peninsula might be required. The nuclear and chemical weapon inspections on the peninsula could be carried out by the IAEA and the OPCW, respectively, while the biological and missile parts would fall under a newly created inspection unit of the Security Council. The experience, institutional memory and archives that were accumulated in UNMOVIC would come to good use.

WMDC RECOMMENDATION

56 The UN Security Council should establish a small subsidiary unit that could provide professional technical information and advice on matters relating to weapons of mass destruction. At the request of the Council or the Secretary-General, it should organize ad hoc inspections and monitoring in the field, using a roster of well-trained inspectors that should be kept up-to-date.

ENFORCEMENT

Treaties on weapons of mass destruction are habitually implemented and respected by the states parties, which are bound by them despite the absence of courts and executive authorities. Yet a state might be tempted to disregard its obligations openly or secretly. What means does the international community have to discourage withdrawals, induce compliance, authoritatively establish whether violations have taken place, and enforce respect for the treaty?

'Enforcement' is not the proper term to describe when actions, perhaps of a military nature, have been taken or threatened to eliminate the suspected existence or development of WMD, regardless of whether there was a violation of a treaty or other legal commitment. The term should be reserved for acts related to the upholding of existing legal obligations by forceful means, political, economic or military. Even when the term is given this more limited meaning, the practical means of 'enforcement' are rather different in the international sphere from those used in ordinary domestic law enforcement.

Enforcement of treaties and other international legal obligations in a community of sovereign states, many of which are economically and militarily powerful, is evidently much more problematic and less certain than enforcement in a national jurisdiction. For arms control and disarmament treaties, questions of enforcement may be referred by an organization or individual states to the UN Security Council, which may both pass judgement and decide on action. A number of points may be noted.

If non-compliance is suspected, attempts must be made to establish this authoritatively through credible investigations. The verification systems operated by the IAEA and the OPCW may provide governments with evidence that may help them to draw convincing conclusions. In other cases, notably suspected breaches of the BWTC, which lacks verification mechanisms of its own, the Security Council could mandate necessary investigations. Any state party may lodge a complaint to the Council about a perceived breach of the treaty and all parties are obliged to cooperate with an investigation initiated by the Council.

Most states in the international community are parties to and stakeholders in the global arms control and disarmament treaties. The rights of each party are affected by the non-compliance of any other party, and each party has a legitimate interest in joining in orderly action to end any non-compliance. Such action may demonstrate that the parties take their commitments seriously and may thus constitute a deterrent against further cases of non-compliance. Enforcement action that is unilateral, or taken by only a few parties without consulting other parties, ignores the responsibility and possible support of other parties and stakeholders. If such action were to involve the use of armed force, it would be subject to the restrictions in the UN Charter.

If the Security Council or another competent body establishes that a state has been non-compliant or that it appears likely or imminent that it will become non-compliant, it should authorize negotiations with a view to ensuring compliance. While it will not be practical to involve all the parties to the relevant treaty, the rights of all are affected. Procedures should be found to consult them and report to them.

Individual WMD treaties and verification agreements contain provisions on measures that can be taken in a case of non-compliance. The IAEA Board of Governors can decide to curtail or suspend assistance to a state and may even suspend the rights and privileges of membership (Article XII.C of the IAEA Statute). Referral to the Security Council is prescribed in some treaties (including the Statute of the IAEA) for some situations, including non-compliance. Moreover, it is always open for member states and the Secretary-General to call the attention of the Council to a situation that, in their view, may threaten international peace and security.

As developed in the next section, the UN Security Council has the power to mandate or authorize a broad array of measures – from negotiations and recommendations to fact finding, intrusive inspections, economic or other sanctions and full-scale military action. While the Council has been given these vast competences, it must exercise them responsibly and with an awareness that it acts on behalf of the whole UN membership. Authorizing armed action against a state on the basis of unsubstantiated allegations or tenuous evidence of non-compliance with a WMD treaty would discredit the Council.

WMDC RECOMMENDATION

57 International legal obligations regarding weapons of mass destruction must be enforced. International enforcement action should be taken only after credible investigation and authoritative finding of non-compliance with legal obligations.

THE ROLE OF THE UNITED NATIONS

Governments are often reluctant to establish new intergovernmental institutions. Officials and political leaders worry that deliberations and decisions on specific matters will move from the national level, which they control, to an international sphere, which they do not. Specific analytical and operational tasks might also pass from national to international institutions.

While some decision makers may fear that such institutions will become too strong, others may believe that they are too weak to be effective – hence they either distrust or are sceptical of such institutions.

Yet leaders of most states also acknowledge that the greatest challenges in the world today, or that are likely to emerge tomorrow, will require extensive cooperation between states. They know that this cooperation will have to be sustained and that it will entail such activities as pooling of information, adopting and maintaining common standards, and managing operations. They know that joint institutions and secretariats are indispensable in performing such roles.

The United Nations disarmament machinery

The current institutional setting for global cooperation relating to WMD was established in 1978 at the first Special Session on Disarmament of the UN General Assembly in 1978. The basic architecture has been the same since then and is often called the UN disarmament 'machinery'. It is one of the two parts of the world's multilateral WMD-relevant institutions – the other part consists of the institutions (described in earlier chapters), which are essential in operating the main WMD treaties, notably the IAEA, the OPCW and the CTBTO.

The UN machinery is often seen as operating at three levels: a deliberative level (the United Nations Disarmament Commission), a consensus-building level (the United Nations General Assembly First Committee) and a body for negotiating treaties (the Conference on Disarmament). At present, all three of these main components of the machinery are plagued to different degrees by political obstacles and blockages.

BOX 27

THE UNITED NATIONS DISARMAMENT 'MACHINERY'

The term 'machinery' was coined in the General Assembly's first Special Session on Disarmament in 1978, whose Final Document has guided multilateral disarmament activities ever since. There is a division of labour between the different parts of the machinery – from the deliberation of basic principles; the preparations, debate, drafting and adoption of resolutions; to the negotiation of multilateral treaties.

The UN Disarmament Commission (UNDC) customarily meets for three weeks each year in New York. All UN member states can participate. The UNDC deliberates basic disarmament concepts and norms. It takes decisions by consensus.

The First Committee of the UN General Assembly in New York considers proposals in the entire field of disarmament and prepares them for vote in the General Assembly. Each year, 40–50 resolutions, which are normative but non-binding, are adopted by majority vote or by consensus.

The Conference on Disarmament (CD) in Geneva serves as the world's single multilateral disarmament negotiating forum. Sixty-five states are currently members, and most other states participate as observers. The CD negotiates multilateral treaties, most recently the CWC and the CTBT, which were concluded in the 1990s. All decisions, both substantive and procedural, must be taken by consensus.

Other institutions include the **UN Department for Disarmament Affairs**, which provides support to the Secretary-General and for important treaties that do not have institutional structures of their own, such as the NPT and the BTWC; and the **United Nations Institute for Disarmament Research (UNIDIR)**, which convenes seminars, undertakes or hosts studies and analyses, and publishes books and reports.

At the opening of the 2000 NPT Review Conference, UN Secretary-General Kofi Annan said:

'Quite frankly, much of the established multilateral machinery has started to rust – a problem due not to the machinery itself but to the apparent lack of political will to use it.'

The United Nations Disarmament Commission (UNDC) is a deliberative body open to all UN member states, which meets annually in New York to consider a limited agenda of disarmament issues and make recommendations, often in the form of guidelines for collective action. It is a subsidiary organ of the General Assembly.

The General Assembly is the most representative body of the world with a responsibility for the area of disarmament. With fresh experience of the standstill, the General Assembly should initiate an effort to revive the disarmament process. Building on the widespread public dismay over the inability of the 2005 World Summit to agree on any reference to WMD issues of disarmament, non-proliferation or terrorism in the 'Outcome Document', the General Assembly should consider calling another World Summit focused on precisely these issues. *The First Committee* of the General Assembly has experienced divisions, best exemplified by the deeply divided votes each year on resolutions dealing with nuclear weapons, most notably nuclear disarmament. While efforts have been under way to reform the working procedures of the First Committee – for example, to introduce fewer resolutions each year and focus more on implementing existing resolutions – they have not been effective.

The Conference on Disarmament has been unable to adopt a Programme of Work for almost a decade. Although there have been some modest improvements in cooperation, the CD remains embroiled in perennial disagreements among blocs of states over basic priorities. Such differences are aggravated and made intractable by the requirement of consensus, a CD rule that applies even to purely procedural decisions, which in practical terms amounts to a right of veto for each member.

In the view of many states, shared by the Commission, this wholesale application of the consensus rule is a relic of the Cold War and should be eliminated. Under this rule, the CD cannot adopt its programme of Work – or other procedural decisions – unless all members agree. By contrast, important decisions of the General Assembly only require a qualified majority of two-thirds of the members present and voting. Many states still benefit from participation in regional groups, but since those were formed during the Cold War, they may have done more to prevent than to facilitate consensus.

WMDC RECOMMENDATION

58

In order for the Conference on Disarmament to function, it should be able to adopt its Programme of Work by a qualified majority of two-thirds of the members present and voting. It should also take its other administrative and procedural decisions with the same requirements.

WMDC RECOMMENDATION

59

The United Nations General Assembly should convene a World Summit on disarmament, non-proliferation and terrorist use of weapons of mass destruction, to meet after thorough preparation. This World Summit should also discuss and decide on reforms to improve the efficiency and effectiveness of the UN disarmament machinery.

The role of the UN Security Council

While the UN General Assembly and organs under it have been deeply engaged in the task of policy-making and negotiations regarding arms control and disarmament (Article 11:1 of the UN Charter), the Security Council has concerned itself principally with specific cases. It has been pragmatic in deciding upon the degree of practical engagement to be taken in the various cases, allowing it to be influenced by the particular circumstances in each case.

Following Iraq's invasion of Kuwait in 1990 and the 1991 Gulf War, the Security Council determined that all Iraq's weapons of mass destruction and missiles of a range greater than 150 km should be eradicated (Security Council Resolution 687). The Council engaged deeply and directly in the process of inspection and disarmament throughout the 1990s and up to and including the Iraq war in 2003.

In the case of North Korea, which was referred to the Council in 1993 by the IAEA Board of Governors on the ground that the country had violated its safeguards agreement, the Council adopted no sanctions but urged its members 'to make appropriate efforts'. In pursuance of this recommendation the US engaged in discussions that in 1994 led to an 'Agreed Framework' with North Korea. The Council took no action on North Korea's notice of withdrawal from the NPT in 2003, and recent efforts to find a solution to the proliferation problems posed by North Korea have been centred on talks in Beijing without any link to the Council.

In 1998, the Council adopted unanimously a resolution condemning the Indian and Pakistani nuclear tests (Resolution 1172).

In 2003, the agreement reached by the US and the UK with Libya about the termination of illegal Libyan programmes of weapons of mass destruction was not reported to the Security Council.

So far in 2006, the world community has been divided about whether or not the Security Council should take action regarding the violations by Iran of its safeguards agreements and the suspicions of an intention on the part of Iran to proceed from a programme of uranium enrichment to a programme of weapon development.

Article 26 of the UN Charter prescribes that the Council shall be responsible for formulating plans for 'the establishment of a system for the regulation of armaments' in order to promote the maintenance of peace and security with the least diversion of resources for armaments, and Article 47:1 makes reference to a 'disarmament' role for the Council. Yet, the Council has not fulfilled this role. While the conditions of the Cold War might explain the passivity in the past it might be questioned whether there is today any good reason why the Council, which comprises as permanent members the states with the world's largest diversion of resources for armaments, should not embark upon the role laid upon it. The question may be the more justified since, in the Post-Cold War period, the Council has gone beyond measures applying to specific cases and made – welcome – efforts to prevent non-nuclear-weapon states and non-state actors from acquiring WMD.

In January 1992, following a summit-level meeting, the Security Council declared through a Presidential Statement that:

'The proliferation of all weapons of mass destruction constitutes a threat to international peace and security. The members of the Council commit themselves to working to prevent the spread of technology related to the research for or production of such weapons and to take appropriate action to that end.'

Under Article 39 of the UN Charter, any determination by the Council that a situation or action constitutes a threat to international peace and security allows the Council to decide under Chapter VII of the Charter on measures, including economic and military sanctions, which are binding. Accordingly, the statement was – and remains – an important signal to the world that the Council will consider itself competent to take a wide range of action in any future case of the proliferation of WMD. Of course, notice that it *can* take action is not the same as notice that it *will* take action. As noted above, the case of Libya's breach of the NPT was not taken to the Council in 2003 but was handled through negotiations between the UK, the US and Libya.

Equally important is the Security Council's adoption of Resolution 1540 in April 2004. Here the position expressed in the Presidential Statement of 1992 was affirmed in a formal Council resolution, which decided with binding effect that all UN member states:

'shall adopt and enforce appropriate effective laws which prohibit any non-state actor to manufacture, acquire, possess, develop, transport, transfer or use nuclear, chemical or biological weapons or their means of delivery in particular for terrorist purposes ...'

In this and other similar resolutions, the Security Council has moved beyond the realm of deciding on measures to be taken by member states in specific cases and prescribed what they must do in a large and diverse category of cases. Moreover, it established machinery to supervise the implementation of the required measures.

The action illustrates the great potential power of the Security Council to deal not only with specific acute cases but also generally with questions of WMD, disarmament, non-proliferation and terrorism – indeed to 'legislate' for the world: member states are obliged under Article 25 of the Charter to accept and carry out the decisions of the Security Council. There is no right of reservation or opting out.

The primary responsibility placed upon the Council for the maintenance of international peace and security is thus matched by the authority that is given to it and that can be exercised to reduce the risk of WMD, whether in the hands of the five permanent members or other members of the United Nations, or non-state actors. This broad authority also raises some questions. It makes the Council legislator, judge and enforcer. All 191 UN member states could become obliged to act in accordance with injunctions that could be decided by as few as nine Council members. Is the Council sufficiently representative of the world to carry such responsibility, or does the composition need to be improved? Do new rules, or at least practices, need to be developed to ensure adequate consultation between the members of the organization that will be bound by decisions, and the members of the Security Council that will take the decisions?

WMDC RECOMMENDATION

60 The United Nations Security Council should make greater use of its potential to reduce and eliminate threats of weapons of mass destruction – whether they are linked to existing arsenals, proliferation or terrorists. It should take up for consideration any withdrawal from or breach of an obligation not to acquire weapons of mass destruction. Making use of its authority under the Charter to take decisions with binding effect for all members, the Council may, *inter alia*:

- require individual states to accept effective and comprehensive monitoring, inspection and verification;
- require member states to enact legislation to secure global implementation of specific rules or measures; and
- decide, as instance of last resort, on the use of economic or military enforcement measures.

Before UN reform has made the Security Council more representative of the UN membership, it is especially important that binding decisions should be preceded by effective consultation to ensure that they are supported by the membership of the UN and will be accepted and respected.

BEYOND WMD

The particular abhorrence of WMD, and the stigma attached to them as weapons of terror, have rightly placed these weapons in the forefront of the arms control and disarmament efforts. This report focuses on how short- and medium-term progress can be made in the effort to outlaw nuclear weapons and to secure full implementation of the prohibitions on biological and chemical weapons. It does not address the even larger question of general and complete disarmament.

The perspective of a world free of WMD must be supplemented by the perspective of a world in which the arsenals of conventional weapons have been reduced drastically. The objective must also be a world in which the international use of armed force, when it becomes necessary, is monopolized by the United Nations (except for self-defence in the case of armed attacks that have occurred or are imminent). It is outside the scope of this report to discuss how this development can be achieved. Only some speculations can be offered.

If the way in which human societies have over time succeeded in limiting the use of armed force and achieving peace in individual nations is any guide, the key factors would seem to be: a measure of economic integration, the establishment of central control over most arms in the territory, protection by the central authority of those who turned in their weapons, and the development of democracy and the rule of law.

It seems improbable that in today's world any single state or group of states would have the will or the power to establish and enforce control over all states and their armed forces. This would not be acceptable to the vast majority of the states in the world.

It is more likely that economic integration, which is accelerating as never before in history, will lead us to even greater interdependence. Tensions between rich and poor societies, the spread of diseases like HIV and avian flu, environmental threats, competition over energy, the functioning of international trade and financial markets, cross-border crime and terrorism, and so forth, will be challenges for all. They will require the development of an international society organized through cooperation and law rather than one controlled by overwhelming military force, including weapons of mass destruction.

Annexes

ANNEX 1: WMDC RECOMMENDATIONS

NUCLEAR WEAPONS

Preventing the proliferation of nuclear weapons

WMDC RECOMMENDATION

1 All parties to the Non-Proliferation Treaty need to revert to the fundamental and balanced non-proliferation and disarmament commitments that were made under the treaty and confirmed in 1995 when the treaty was extended indefinitely.

WMDC RECOMMENDATION

2 All parties to the Non-Proliferation Treaty should implement the decision on principles and objectives for non-proliferation and disarmament, the decision on strengthening the Non-Proliferation Treaty review process, and the resolution on the Middle East as a zone free of nuclear and all other weapons of mass destruction, all adopted in 1995. They should also promote the implementation of 'the thirteen practical steps' for nuclear disarmament that were adopted in 2000.

WMDC RECOMMENDATION

3 To enhance the effectiveness of the nuclear non-proliferation regime, all Non-Proliferation Treaty non-nuclear-weapon states parties should accept comprehensive safeguards as strengthened by the International Atomic Energy Agency Additional Protocol.

WMDC RECOMMENDATION

4 The states parties to the Non-Proliferation Treaty should establish a standing secretariat to handle administrative matters for the parties to the treaty. This secretariat should organize the treaty's Review Conferences and their Preparatory Committee sessions. It should also organize other treaty-related meetings upon the request of a majority of the states parties.

WMDC RECOMMENDATION

5 Negotiations with North Korea should aim at a verifiable agreement including, as a principal element, North Korea's manifesting its adherence to the Non-Proliferation Treaty and accepting the 1997 Additional Protocol, as well as revival and legal confirmation of the commitments made in the 1992 Joint Declaration on the Denuclearization of the Korean Peninsula: notably, that neither North nor South Korea shall have nuclear weapons or nuclear reprocessing and uranium enrichment facilities. Fuel-cycle services should be assured through international arrangements. The agreement should also cover biological and chemical weapons, as well as the Comprehensive Nuclear-Test-Ban Treaty, thus making the Korean peninsula a zone free of weapons of mass destruction.

WMDC RECOMMENDATION

6 Negotiations must be continued to induce Iran to suspend any sensitive fuel-cycle-related activities and ratify the 1997 Additional Protocol and resume full cooperation with the International Atomic Energy Agency in order to avoid an increase in tensions and to improve the outlook for the common aim of establishing a Middle East zone free of weapons of mass destruction. The international community and Iran should build mutual confidence through measures that should include: reliable assurance regarding the supply of fuel-cycle services; suspending or renouncing sensitive fuel-cycle activities for a prolonged period of time by all states in the Middle East; assurances against attacks and subversion aiming at regime change; and facilitation of international trade and investment.

WMDC RECOMMENDATION

7 The nuclear-weapon states parties to the Non-Proliferation Treaty should provide legally binding negative security assurances to non-nuclear-weapon states parties. The states not party to the Non-Proliferation Treaty that possess nuclear weapons should separately provide such assurances.

WMDC RECOMMENDATION

8 States should make active use of the IAEA as a forum for exploring various ways to reduce proliferation risks connected with the nuclear fuel cycle, such as proposals for an international fuel bank; internationally safeguarded regional centres offering fuel-cycle services, including spent-fuel repositories; and the creation of a fuel-cycle system built on the concept that a few 'fuel-cycle states' will lease nuclear fuel to states that forgo enrichment and reprocessing activities.

WMDC RECOMMENDATION

9 States should develop means of using low-enriched uranium in ships and research reactors that presently require highly enriched uranium. The production of highly enriched uranium should be phased out. States that separate plutonium by reprocessing spent nuclear fuel should explore possibilities for reducing that activity.

WMDC RECOMMENDATION

10 All states should support the international initiatives taken to advance the global clean-out of fissile material. Such support should encompass the conversion of research reactors from highly enriched to low-enriched uranium fuel, storing fissile material at centralized and secure locations, and returning exported nuclear materials to suppliers for secure disposal or elimination.

WMDC RECOMMENDATION

11 All Non-Proliferation Treaty nuclear-weapon states that have not yet done so should ratify the protocols of the treaties creating regional nuclear-weapon-free zones. All states in such zones should conclude their comprehensive safeguards agreements with the IAEA and agree to ratify and implement the Additional Protocol.

WMDC RECOMMENDATION

12

All states should support continued efforts to establish a zone free of weapons of mass destruction in the Middle East as a part of the overall peace process. Steps can be taken even now. As a confidence-building measure, all states in the region, including Iran and Israel, should for a prolonged period of time commit themselves to a verified arrangement not to have any enrichment, reprocessing or other sensitive fuel-cycle activities on their territories. Such a commitment should be coupled with reliable assurances about fuel-cycle services required for peaceful nuclear activities. Egypt, Iran and Israel should join the other states in the Middle East in ratifying the CTBT.

WMDC RECOMMENDATION

13

India and Pakistan should both ratify the CTBT and join those other states with nuclear weapons that have declared a moratorium on the production of fissile material for weapons, pending the conclusion of a treaty. They should continue to seek bilateral détente and build confidence through political, economic and military measures, reducing the risk of armed conflict, and increasing transparency in the nuclear and missile activities of both countries. Eventually, both states should become members of the Nuclear Suppliers Group and the Missile Technology Control Regime, as well as parties to International Atomic Energy Agency safeguards agreements under the terms of the 1997 Additional Protocol.

Preventing nuclear terrorism

WMDC RECOMMENDATION

14 States must prevent terrorists from gaining access to nuclear weapons or fissile material. To achieve this, they must maintain fully effective accounting and control of all stocks of fissile and radioactive material and other radiological sources on their territories. They should ensure that there is personal legal responsibility for any acts of nuclear terrorism or activities in support of such terrorism. They must expand their cooperation through *inter alia* the sharing of information, including intelligence on illicit nuclear commerce. They should also promote universal adherence to the International Convention for the Suppression of Acts of Nuclear Terrorism and to the Convention on the Physical Protection of Nuclear Material and implementation of UN Security Council Resolution 1540.

Reducing the threat and the numbers of existing nuclear weapons

WMDC RECOMMENDATION

15 All states possessing nuclear weapons should declare a categorical policy of no-first-use of such weapons. They should specify that this covers both pre-emptive and preventive action, as well as retaliation for attacks involving chemical, biological or conventional weapons.

WMDC RECOMMENDATION

16 All states possessing nuclear weapons should review their military plans and define what is needed to maintain credible non-nuclear security policies. States deploying their nuclear forces in triads, consisting of submarine-launched missiles, ground-based intercontinental ballistic missiles and long-range bombers, should abandon this practice in order to reduce nuclear-weapon redundancy and avoid fuelling nuclear arms races.

WMDC RECOMMENDATION

17 Russia and the United States should agree on reciprocal steps to take their nuclear weapons off hair-trigger alert and should create a joint commission to facilitate this goal. They should undertake to eliminate the launch-on-warning option from their nuclear war plans, while implementing a controlled parallel decrease in operational readiness of a large part of their strategic forces, through:

- reducing the number of strategic submarines at sea and lowering their technical readiness to launch while in port;
- storing nuclear bombs and air-launched cruise missiles separately from relevant air fields;
- storing separately nose cones and/or warheads of most inter-continental ballistic missiles or taking other technical measures to reduce their readiness.

WMDC RECOMMENDATION

18 Russia and the United States should commence negotiations on a new strategic arms reduction treaty aimed at reducing their deployments of strategic forces allowed under the Strategic Offensive Reductions Treaty by at least half. It should include a legally binding commitment to irreversibly dismantle the weapons withdrawn under the Strategic Offensive Reductions Treaty. The new treaty should also include transparent counting rules, schedules and procedures for dismantling the weapons, and reciprocal measures for verification.

WMDC RECOMMENDATION

19 Russia and the United States, followed by other states possessing nuclear weapons, should publish their aggregate holdings of nuclear weapons on active and reserve status as a baseline for future disarmament efforts. They should also agree to include specific provisions in future disarmament agreements relating to transparency, irreversibility, verification and the physical destruction of nuclear warheads.

WMDC RECOMMENDATION

20

All states possessing nuclear weapons must address the issue of their continued possession of such weapons. All nuclear-weapon states parties to the Non-Proliferation Treaty must take steps towards nuclear disarmament, as required by the treaty and the commitments made in connection with the treaty's indefinite extension. Russia and the United States should take the lead. Other states possessing nuclear weapons should join the process, individually or in coordinated action. While Israel, India and Pakistan are not parties to the Non-Proliferation Treaty, they, too, have a duty to contribute to the nuclear disarmament process.

WMDC RECOMMENDATION

21

Russia and the United States should proceed to implement the commitments they made in 1991 to eliminate specific types of non-strategic nuclear weapons, such as demolition munitions, artillery shells and warheads for short-range ballistic missiles. They should agree to withdraw all non-strategic nuclear weapons to central storage on national territory, pending their eventual elimination. The two countries should reinforce their 1991 unilateral reduction commitments by developing arrangements to ensure verification, transparency and irreversibility.

WMDC RECOMMENDATION

22

Every state that possesses nuclear weapons should make a commitment not to deploy any nuclear weapon, of any type, on foreign soil.

WMDC RECOMMENDATION

23

Any state contemplating replacement or modernization of its nuclear-weapon systems must consider such action in the light of all relevant treaty obligations and its duty to contribute to the nuclear disarmament process. As a minimum, it must refrain from developing nuclear weapons with new military capabilities or for new missions. It must not adopt systems or doctrines that blur the distinction between nuclear and conventional weapons or lower the nuclear threshold.

WMDC RECOMMENDATION

24 All states possessing nuclear weapons, notably Russia and the United States, should place their excess fissile material from military programmes under International Atomic Energy Agency safeguards. To facilitate the reduction of stocks of highly enriched uranium, states possessing such stocks should sell uranium blended to enrichment levels suitable for reactor fuel to other Non-Proliferation Treaty states or use it for their own peaceful nuclear energy needs.

WMDC RECOMMENDATION

25 All states possessing nuclear weapons should adopt strict standards for the handling of weapons-usable fissile material deemed excess to military requirements or recovered from disarmament activities, as exemplified in the US stored-weapon and spent-fuel standards.

WMDC RECOMMENDATION

26 The Conference on Disarmament should immediately open the delayed negotiations for a treaty on the cut-off of production of fissile material for weapons without preconditions. Before, or at least during, these negotiations, the Conference on Disarmament should establish a Group of Scientific Experts to examine technical aspects of the treaty.

WMDC RECOMMENDATION

27 To facilitate fissile material cut-off negotiations in the Conference on Disarmament, the five Non-Proliferation Treaty nuclear-weapon states, joined by the other states possessing nuclear weapons, should agree among themselves to cease production of fissile material for weapon purposes. They should open up their facilities for such production to International Atomic Energy Agency safeguards inspections, building on the practice of Euratom inspections in France and the UK. These eight states should also address the issue of verifiable limitations of existing stocks of weapons-usable nuclear materials.

WMDC RECOMMENDATION

28

All states that have not already done so should sign and ratify the Comprehensive Nuclear-Test-Ban Treaty unconditionally and without delay. The United States, which has not ratified the treaty, should reconsider its position and proceed to ratify the treaty, recognizing that its ratification would trigger other required ratifications and be a step towards the treaty's entry into force. Pending entry into force, all states with nuclear weapons should continue to refrain from nuclear testing. Also, the 2007 conference of Comprehensive Nuclear-Test-Ban Treaty signatories should address the possibility of a provisional entry into force of the treaty.

WMDC RECOMMENDATION

29

All signatories should provide financial, political and technical support for the continued development and operation of the verification regime, including the International Monitoring System, the International Data Centre and the secretariat, so that the CTBTO is ready to monitor and verify compliance with the treaty when it enters into force. They should pledge to maintain their respective stations and continue to transmit data on a national basis under all circumstances.

From regulating nuclear weapons to outlawing them

WMDC RECOMMENDATION

30

All states possessing nuclear weapons should commence planning for security without nuclear weapons. They should start preparing for the outlawing of nuclear weapons through joint practical and incremental measures that include definitions, benchmarks and transparency requirements for nuclear disarmament.

BIOLOGICAL AND TOXIN WEAPONS

WMDC RECOMMENDATION

31 All states not yet party to the Biological and Toxin Weapons Convention should adhere to the Convention. The states parties to the Convention should launch a campaign to achieve universal adherence by the time of the Seventh Review Conference, to be held in 2011.

WMDC RECOMMENDATION

32 To achieve universal adoption of national legislation and regulations to implement the Biological and Toxin Weapons Convention completely and effectively, the states parties should offer technical assistance and promote best-practice models of such legislation. As a part of the confidence-building process and to promote transparency and harmonization, all states parties should make annual biological-weapon-related national declarations and make them public.

WMDC RECOMMENDATION

33 States parties to the Biological and Toxin Weapons Convention should enhance the investigatory powers of the UN Secretary-General, ensuring that the Secretary-General's office can rely upon a regularly updated roster of experts and advice from the World Health Organization and a specialist unit, modelled on the United Nations Monitoring, Verification and Inspection Commission, to assist in investigating unusual outbreaks of disease and allegations of the use of biological weapons.

WMDC RECOMMENDATION

34 States parties to the Biological and Toxin Weapons Convention should establish a standing secretariat to handle organizational and administrative matters related to the treaty, such as Review Conferences and expert meetings.

WMDC RECOMMENDATION

35 Governments should pursue public health surveillance to ensure effective monitoring of unusual outbreaks of disease and develop practical methods of coordinating international responses to any major event that might involve bioweapons. They should strengthen cooperation between civilian health and security-oriented authorities, nationally, regionally and worldwide, including in the framework of the new International Health Regulations of the World Health Organization. Governments should also review their national biosafety and biosecurity measures to protect health and the environment from the release of biological and toxin materials. They should harmonize national biosecurity standards.

WMDC RECOMMENDATION

36 At the Sixth Review Conference, in 2006, the states parties to the Biological and Toxin Weapons Convention should reaffirm common understandings reached at previous review conferences and take action on all subjects addressed at Convention meetings since 2003. They should also establish a work programme on additional topics for future meetings. States parties should ensure more frequent reassessment of the implications of scientific and technological developments and reaffirm that all undertakings under Article I of the Biological and Toxin Weapons Convention apply to such developments. This Review Conference should reaffirm that all developments in the life sciences fall within the scope of the Convention and that all developments in the life sciences for hostile purposes are prohibited by the Convention.

CHEMICAL WEAPONS

WMDC RECOMMENDATION

37 States parties to the Chemical Weapons Convention must provide adequate resources to ensure that there are no undue delays in the agreed destruction of chemical weapon stockpiles.

WMDC RECOMMENDATION

38 The Organisation for the Prohibition of Chemical Weapons and states parties to the Chemical Weapons Convention should continue their efforts to secure universal adherence to the Convention. States parties should fully implement the rules on trade and transfer of chemicals that are precursors to chemical-weapon agents. They should further develop regulations regarding the trade and transfer of chemicals that can be used to produce chemical weapons. The Organisation for the Prohibition of Chemical Weapons and states parties should continue to offer states positive incentives, including technical assistance, to join and implement the Chemical Weapons Convention. When providing such assistance or transferring relevant technologies, they should consider steps to ensure safe and responsible handling by the recipient.

WMDC RECOMMENDATION

39 States parties to the Chemical Weapons Convention should confirm that, like the use of riot control agents, the use of toxic chemical agents for purposes of law enforcement is banned as a method of warfare. Accordingly, each state party must declare any such agent under Article III.

WMDC RECOMMENDATION

40 States parties should ensure that the Organisation for the Prohibition of Chemical Weapons has the resources, experience and legal rights needed to carry out challenge inspections in a timely and effective manner, including for the taking of samples and removal of samples for testing.

WMDC RECOMMENDATION

41 Through their domestic laws and policies, all states should prohibit the production, possession and use of toxic chemicals and technologies for purposes that are banned by the Chemical Weapons Convention. States should ensure security in and for chemical facilities through legislation and agreement with industry. States should also develop national means to monitor that security standards are met.

WMDC RECOMMENDATION 42

42 States parties to the Chemical Weapons Convention should use the Organisation for the Prohibition of Chemical Weapons as a coordinating centre in the development of global standards for a chemical industry security culture. The Organisation should offer evaluation and security assistance at declared sites. States parties should also strengthen the capacity of the Organisation for the Prohibition of Chemical Weapons to provide practical assistance against chemical weapons, for instance detection equipment, alarm systems and medical antidotes.

WMD DELIVERY MEANS, MISSILE DEFENCES, AND WEAPONS IN SPACE

WMDC RECOMMENDATION

43 MTCR member states should make new efforts to better implement and expand export controls on relevant materials and technology. States subscribing to the Hague Code of Conduct should extend its scope to include cruise missiles and unmanned aerial vehicles. They should establish a multilateral data exchange centre, based on the Russian-US initiatives for the exchange of data on missile launches from early-warning systems. Regional and international non-proliferation measures should include information exchanges, launch notification, and restrictions or bans on specific items or capabilities.

WMDC RECOMMENDATION 44

44 States should not consider the deployment or further deployment of any kind of missile defence system without first attempting to negotiate the removal of missile threats. If such negotiations fail, deployments of such systems should be accompanied by cooperative development programmes and confidence-building measures to lower the risk of adverse effects on international peace and security, including the risk of creating or aggravating arms races.

WMDC RECOMMENDATION 45

45 All states should renounce the deployment of weapons in outer space. They should promote universal adherence to the Outer Space Treaty and expand its scope through a protocol to prohibit all weapons in space. Pending the conclusion of such a protocol, they should refrain from activities inconsistent with its aims, including any tests against space objects or targets on earth from a space platform. States should adapt the international regimes and institutions for space issues so that both military and civilian aspects can be dealt with in the same context. States should also set up a group of experts to develop options for monitoring and verifying various components of a space security regime and a code of conduct, designed *inter alia* to prohibit the testing or deployment of space weapons.

WMDC RECOMMENDATION

46 A Review Conference of the Outer Space Treaty to mark its 40th year in force should be held in 2007. It should address the need to strengthen the treaty and extend its scope. A Special Coordinator should be appointed to facilitate ratifications and liaise with non-parties about the reinforcement of the treaty-based space security regime.

EXPORT CONTROLS, INTERNATIONAL ASSISTANCE, AND NON-GOVERNMENTAL ACTORS

WMDC RECOMMENDATION

47 All states should conduct audits of their export control enforcement agencies (customs, police, coastguard, border control and military) to ensure that they can carry out their tasks effectively. States should seek to establish a universal system of export controls providing harmonized standards, enhanced transparency, and practical support for implementation. Members of the five export control regimes should promote a widening of their membership and improve implementation in view of current security challenges, without impeding legitimate trade and economic development.

WMDC RECOMMENDATION

48
The G8 Global Partnership should expand the geographical and functional scope of its non-proliferation assistance. The G8 should guarantee full funding for the Elimination of Weapons-Grade Plutonium Production (EWGPP) programme. Potential donors should consider how technical assistance, training, equipment and financing could be brought to bear to help states of all regions implement UN Security Council Resolution 1540.

WMDC RECOMMENDATION

49
Companies engaged in activities relevant to weapons of mass destruction have the ability and responsibility to help prevent the proliferation of such weapons and an interest in demonstrating that they are fulfilling that responsibility, including full compliance with national and international obligations and public transparency. Trade associations should promote such objectives.

WMDC RECOMMENDATION

50
States, international organizations and professional associations should encourage the appropriate academic and industrial associations to adopt and effectively implement codes of practice and codes of conduct for science and research in weapons of mass destruction-relevant fields.

WMDC RECOMMENDATION

51
Governments possessing any weapons of mass destruction should keep their parliaments fully and currently informed of their holdings of such weapons and their activities to reduce and eliminate them. Parliaments should actively seek such information and recognize their responsibility in formulating policies relevant to weapons of mass destruction issues. Greater inter-parliamentary cooperation on weapons of mass destruction issues is needed.

WMDC RECOMMENDATION

52
States should assist Non-Governmental Organizations to actively participate in international meetings and conferences, and to inform and campaign in the weapons of mass destruction field. Private foundations should substantially increase their support for such organizations that are working to eliminate global weapons of mass destruction threats.

WMDC RECOMMENDATION

53

Organizations with security-relevant agendas should re-examine the 2002 United Nations Study on Disarmament and Non-Proliferation Education, and should consider ways in which they could foster and support such education and an informed public debate. Governments should fund student internships at multilateral institutions working on weapons of mass destruction issues.

COMPLIANCE, VERIFICATION, ENFORCEMENT AND THE ROLE OF THE UNITED NATIONS

WMDC RECOMMENDATION

54

As the strengthened safeguards system adopted by the International Atomic Energy Agency through the Additional Protocol should become standard for parties to the Non-Proliferation Treaty, supplier states should make acceptance of this standard by recipient parties a condition for contracts involving nuclear items.

WMDC RECOMMENDATION

55

Governments should instruct their intelligence authorities to assist international inspection agencies by providing relevant information without compromising the independence of the inspection systems.

WMDC RECOMMENDATION

56

The UN Security Council should establish a small subsidiary unit that could provide professional technical information and advice on matters relating to weapons of mass destruction. At the request of the Council or the Secretary-General, it should organize ad hoc inspections and monitoring in the field, using a roster of well-trained inspectors that should be kept up-to-date.

WMDC RECOMMENDATION

57

International legal obligations regarding weapons of mass destruction must be enforced. International enforcement action should be taken only after credible investigation and authoritative finding of non-compliance with legal obligations.

WMDC RECOMMENDATION

58 In order for the Conference on Disarmament to function, it should be able to adopt its Programme of Work by a qualified majority of two-thirds of the members present and voting. It should also take its other administrative and procedural decisions with the same requirements.

WMDC RECOMMENDATION

59 The United Nations General Assembly should convene a World Summit on disarmament, non-proliferation and terrorist use of weapons of mass destruction, to meet after thorough preparations. This World Summit should also discuss and decide on reforms to improve the efficiency and effectiveness of the UN disarmament machinery.

WMDC RECOMMENDATION

60 The United Nations Security Council should make greater use of its potential to reduce and eliminate threats of weapons of mass destruction – whether they are linked to existing arsenals, proliferation or terrorists. It should take up for consideration any withdrawal from or breach of an obligation not to acquire weapons of mass destruction. Making use of its authority under the Charter to take decisions with binding effect for all members, the Council may, *inter alia*:

- require individual states to accept effective and comprehensive monitoring, inspection and verification;
- require member states to enact legislation to secure global implementation of specific rules or measures; and
- decide, as instance of last resort, on the use of economic or military enforcement measures.

Before UN reform has made the Security Council more representative of the UN membership, it is especially important that binding decisions should be preceded by effective consultation to ensure that they are supported by the membership of the UN and will be accepted and respected.

ANNEX 2: WORK OF THE COMMISSION

Mandate of the Commission

(As adopted by the Commission on 28 January 2004)

Background

The Weapons of Mass Destruction Commission (WMDC) is established on an initiative by the late Foreign Minister of Sweden, Anna Lindh, acting on a proposal by then United Nations Under-Secretary-General Jayantha Dhanapala. The Swedish Government invited Dr. Hans Blix to set up and chair the Commission. He presented the composition of the Commission to the public on 16 December 2003 and explained what he saw were major tasks for it.

The Commission commences its work against the background of more than a half-century's striving for non-proliferation, arms control and disarmament of weapons of mass destruction. While there has been much success and progress, especially after the end of the Cold War, there have been many difficulties and disappointments in recent years. The technical evolution and the access to knowledge have also reduced some barriers to the acquisition of weapons. The possession and potential use of weapons of mass destruction by states or non-state actors remain ever-present risks. The slowdown and stalemate in the fields of non-proliferation, arms control and disarmament needs to be reversed and the momentum needs to be regained. Major contributions to national and international security would result.

The Commission's task

The Commission should seek to identify desirable and achievable directions for international cooperation. It should present realistic proposals aimed at the greatest possible reduction of the dangers of weapons of mass destruction. These should comprise both short-term and long-term approaches and aim at preventing the further spread of weapons as well as at their reduction and elimination. The scope of the investigation should be comprehensive and include nuclear, biological, chemical and radiological weapons and the means of delivering them, as well as possible links between these issues and terrorists.

The Commission should not be engaged in any tasks or negotiations at the governmental or intergovernmental level.

The Commission should help to stimulate an informed public debate about international and national efforts against weapons of mass destruction. It should therefore undertake outreach activities within its capacity to engage civil society and non-governmental organisations.

Independence

The Commission is fully independent.

The Commissioners have been invited by the Chairman to serve in their personal capacity. They do not serve under instructions from any government or organisation.

While the Secretariat submits accounts for auditing by the Swedish Government, which is providing major funds, in its substantive work it is independent of all Governments and international organisations and non-governmental organisations.

Funding policy

The Commission is funded by the Swedish Government. Contributions from other governmental or private sources are welcomed.

Neither the funding from the Swedish Government nor any other contributions will be allowed to influence the substantive work of, or the final report of, the Commission.

Secretariat

The Commission's secretariat is based in Stockholm. It will engage with expertise from around the world, as instructed or authorised by the Commission or its Chairman.

The Secretariat receives its instructions from the Commission through its Chairman.

Commissioners' biographies

Chairman of the Commission:

HANS BLIX

Before joining the Swedish Ministry for Foreign Affairs, Dr Blix was Associate Professor in International Law at Stockholm University. From 1963 to 1976 he served as the Adviser on International Law in the Ministry. In 1976–78 he was State Secretary for International Development Co-operation and in 1978–79 Minister for Foreign Affairs. He served as Director General of the International Atomic Energy Agency (IAEA), Vienna, from 1981 to 1997 and as Executive Chairman of the UN Monitoring, Verification and Inspection Commission (UNMOVIC) from March 2000 to June 2003. Dr Blix has written several books on subjects associated with international and constitutional law and international affairs.

Commissioners:

DEWI FORTUNA ANWAR

Dr Anwar is Deputy Chair for Social Sciences and Humanities at the Indonesian Institute of Sciences. She is also Director for Research and Program at the Habibie Center in Jakarta and a member of the Board of Directors of the Center for Information and Development Studies. Dr Anwar held the positions of Assistant to the Vice-President for Global Affairs and Assistant Minister/State Secretary for Foreign Affairs during the Habibie Administration. Dr Anwar has worked as a Research Fellow at the Institute of South Asian Studies in Singapore and as a Congressional Fellow at the US Congress in Washington, DC.

ALEXEI G. ARBATOV

Dr Arbatov is a corresponding member of the Russian Academy of Sciences and the Director of Center for International Security at the Institute for World Economy and International Relations (IMEMO). He is also a member of the Advisory Council of the Russian Foreign Minister and a Professor of the Russian Academy on Defence and Security chaired by the President of the Russian Federation. Dr Arbatov is an associate scholar of the Carnegie Foundation. In 1993–2003, Dr Arbatov served as a Deputy Chairman of the Defence Committee of the State Duma of the Federal Assembly of the Russian Federation. Before taking his seat in the Duma, Dr Arbatov headed the

Department on Disarmament and Security of IMEMO, an institute he had originally joined as a researcher in international relations in 1973. He is a member of the Governing Board of SIPRI (Stockholm International Peace Research Institute) and a member of the International Advisory Council of Geneva Centre of Democratic Control of Armed Forces.

MARCOS DE AZAMBUJA

Ambassador de Azambuja was previously Permanent Representative of Brazil to the United Nations and the Conference on Disarmament in Geneva and served as ambassador in France and Argentina. Ambassador de Azambuja has also held the position of Secretary-General of the Ministry of Foreign Relations in Brazil. He served as a member of the Tokyo Forum 1998–99 which produced the report 'Facing Nuclear Dangers – An Action Plan for the 21st Century', with proposals on nuclear non-proliferation and disarmament, which was later submitted to the UN Secretary-General.

ALYSON J. K. BAILES

Alyson J.K. Bailes is the Director of the Stockholm International Peace Research Institute (SIPRI). She served for 32 years in the British diplomatic service, many of the positions involving arms control, security policy and defence-related matters. From 1987 until 1990 she served as Deputy Head of Mission at the Embassy in Beijing, being actively involved in the negotiations on Hong Kong. In 1994–1996 she was head of the FCO Security Policy Department and in 1997–2000 Political Director of the Brussels-based defence institution Western European Union. In 2000 she was appointed Ambassador to Finland, a position she held until 2002 when she resigned from the diplomatic service to take up her current position at SIPRI.

JAYANTHA DHANAPALA

Ambassador Dhanapala was UN Under-Secretary-General for Disarmament Affairs in 1998–2003 and the President of the 1995 NPT Review and Extension Conference. Ambassador Dhanapala joined the Sri Lanka Foreign Service in 1965 and has served in London, Beijing, Washington, DC, and New Delhi. In 1984 he was appointed Ambassador to the United Nations in Geneva and in 1987 left the Foreign Service to head the United Nations Institute for Disarmament Research (UNIDIR). In 1992 he returned to the Foreign Service as Additional Foreign Secretary before taking up the position of Ambassador to the United States. He has also served as Commissioner in UNSCOM, the Head of the Special Group visiting the Presidential Sites in

Iraq, and a member of the 1996 Canberra Commission on the Elimination of Nuclear Weapons. Ambassador Dhanapala has published four books and several articles and is the recipient of four honorary doctorates and several international awards.

GARETH EVANS

Gareth Evans has been President and Chief Executive of the Brussels-based International Crisis Group since January 2000. An Australian Senator and MP from 1978 to 1999, and a Cabinet Minister for 13 years (1983–96), as Foreign Minister (1988–96) he played prominent roles in developing the UN peace plan for Cambodia, concluding the Chemical Weapons Convention, founding the Asia Pacific Economic Cooperation (APEC) forum and initiating the Canberra Commission on the Elimination of Nuclear Weapons. His many publications include *Cooperating for Peace* (1993) and the articles 'Cooperative Security and Intrastate Conflict' (*Foreign Policy*, 1994) and 'The Responsibility to Protect' (*Foreign Affairs*, 2002). He served as Co-chair of the International Commission on Intervention and State Sovereignty and was also a member of the UN Secretary-General's High-level Panel on Threats, Challenges and Change.

PATRICIA LEWIS

Dr Lewis is Director of the United Nations Institute for Disarmament Research (UNIDIR). Formerly she was the Director of the Verification Technology and Information Centre (VERTIC) in London from 1989 to 1997. Dr Lewis was appointed UK Governmental Expert to the 1990 UN study on the role of the UN in verification and also worked as a consultant on conventional forces verification with the UK Foreign Commonwealth Office. She served as a member of the Tokyo Forum in 1998–99 and an external reviewer for the 1996 Canberra Commission. Dr Lewis holds a BSc in physics and a PhD in nuclear physics.

MASASHI NISHIHARA

Dr Nishihara is currently Director of the Japanese Research Institute for Peace and Security. Until March 2006, he was President of the National Defence Academy. Prior to that he was Professor of International Relations at the Academy. He has also served as Director of the First Research Department of the National Institute for Defence Studies in Tokyo.

WILLIAM J. PERRY

Dr Perry was United States Secretary of Defense from February 1994 to January 1997. Prior to that he served as Deputy Secretary of Defense. Dr Perry is currently professor at Stanford University with joint appointment in the School of Engineering and the Institute for International Studies, and is co-director of the joint Harvard-Stanford Preventive Defense Project.

VASANTHA RAGHAVAN

V. R. Raghavan is the Director of the Delhi Policy Group, and President, Centre for Security Analysis, Chennai. A retired Lieutenant-General, Mr Raghavan is a Council Member of the International Institute for Strategic Studies, London.

CHEIKH SYLLA

Ambassador Sylla serves as Senegal's ambassador to Burkina Faso. He has served as Commissioner to the UN Monitoring, Verification and Inspection Commission (UNMOVIC). Ambassador Sylla was a member of the Group of Experts which drafted the Treaty of Pelindaba – making Africa a nuclear-weapon-free zone and also a member of the Group of Experts to carry out the UN Study of Nuclear Weapons in All Their Aspects.

PRINCE EL HASSAN BIN TALAL

Prince El Hassan is Chairman of the Arab Thought Forum, President of the Club of Rome, Moderator of the World Conference for the World Intellectual Property Organization, Founding Member, Vice-Chairman of the Foundation for Interreligious and Intercultural Research and Dialogue. He is also Member of the Board of Trustees of the International Crisis Group and co-chair of the Independent Commission on International Humanitarian Issues.

PAN, ZHENQIANG

Mr Pan, Zhenqiang is Vice-President of the China Foundation for International Studies and Academic Changes. A retired Major-General of the People's Liberation Army, he is also former Director of the Institute of Strategic Studies, National Defence University of China, Beijing. He is active in the Pugwash movement.

THÉRÈSE DELPECH, Director for Strategic Affairs at the Atomic Energy Commission, Paris, was a member of the Commission January 2004–August 2005.

Secretariat

Henrik Salander, Secretary-General
Birgitta Gradin, Administrative Officer
Daniel Nord, Expert (through August 2005)
Manne Wängborg, Senior Adviser (November 2004–March 2006),
    Deputy Secretary-General (from April 2006)
Randy Rydell, Senior Counsellor and Report Director (from January 2005)
Stig Berglind, Media Relations (from January 2006)

Financial and organizational support

The Swedish Ministry for Foreign Affairs has initiated the WMDC and been the financial backbone of the project. The Simons Foundation of Vancouver, Canada, made an early commitment to it and has provided generous financial and organizational support throughout the process.

The Commission has fruitfully co-operated with and received organizational support from, *inter alia*, the Arms Control Association, Washington, D.C.; Federal Ministry of Foreign Affairs, Austria; Ministry of External Relations and Foreign Trade, Canada; Delhi Policy Group, New Delhi; Egyptian Council for Foreign Affairs, Cairo, Egypt; Ministry for Foreign Affairs, Finland; Friedrich Ebert Stiftung, Germany; International Institute for International Affairs, London; Ministry of Foreign Affairs and Trade, New Zealand; Nixon Center, Washington, D.C.; Ministry of Foreign Affairs, Norway; Norwegian Institute of International Affairs, Oslo; Norwegian Radiation Protection Authority, Oslo; Pugwash Conferences on Science and World Affairs, Rome/Washington/London; The Swedish Network for Nuclear Disarmament, Stockholm; and Federal Department of Foreign Affairs, Switzerland.

The Commission would like to express its deep gratitude to all that have sponsored it financially, supported it organizationally and co-operated with it practically in joint endeavours.

Acknowledgements

The Commission has received advice and support from many individuals, institutes and organizations the world over, including those that have authored or contributed to the published WMDC studies listed below. Without their generous cooperation and professional advice this report would not have been possible. The Commission's sincere appreciation is extended to all of them. In addition, the Commission would like to acknowledge its gratitude to Dr Eileen Choffnes, Institute of Medicine, US National Academy of Sciences; Dr Britta Häggström, Division of NBC Defence, Swedish Defence Research Agency (FOI); Dr Rebecca Johnson, Executive Director of the Acronym Institute, who generously contributed her expertise from the initiation of the Commission and continued to support its work with dedication and professional advice; Dr Milton Leitenberg, Senior Research Scholar, University of Maryland; Mr. Sverre Lodgaard, Director, The Norwegian Institute of International Affairs; Mr. Jan Prawitz, Swedish Institute of International Affairs; and Professor John Simpson, Mountbatten Centre for International Studies. They are in no way accountable for any mistakes, errors and other inadequacies in the report; the Commission, of course, accepts full responsibility for the contents and recommendations of the report.

Commission's sessions

First meeting of the Weapons of Mass Destruction Commission
Stockholm, Sweden, 28–30 January 2004

Second meeting of the Weapons of Mass Destruction Commission
Vienna, Austria, 28–30 June 2004

Third meeting of the Weapons of Mass Destruction Commission
Vancouver, Canada, 9–11 November 2004

Fourth meeting of the Weapons of Mass Destruction Commission
Cairo, Egypt, 31 January–2 February 2005

Fifth meeting of the Weapons of Mass Destruction Commission
New Delhi, India, 14–16 March 2005

Sixth meeting of the Weapons of Mass Destruction Commission
Stockholm, Sweden, 11–13 June 2005

Seventh meeting of the Weapons of Mass Destruction Commission
Geneva, Switzerland, 5–7 September 2005

Eighth meeting of the Weapons of Mass Destruction Commission
Stockholm, Sweden, 10–12 November 2005

Ninth meeting of the Weapons of Mass Destruction Commission
Stockholm, Sweden, 16–18 January 2006

Tenth meeting of the Weapons of Mass Destruction Commission
Stockholm, Sweden, 3–5 March 2006

Seminars and other public meetings

As part of its outreach efforts, the Commission has organized a number of seminars, panels and other public meetings, *inter alia*:

Weapons of Mass Destruction Elimination: A Middle Eastern Perspective
Time: 29–30 January 2005
Venue: The Diplomatic Club, Cairo, Egypt
Organizer: A joint meeting of the Weapons of Mass Destruction Commission, Egyptian Council for Foreign Affairs, Pugwash Conferences on Science and World Affairs and the Friedrich Ebert Stiftung.

Reaching Nuclear Disarmament: New Challenges and Possibilities
A conference on new challenges and possibilities for nuclear disarmament in the current political environment. Focus was on issues related to the NPT and also the work of the WMDC.
Time: 25–27 February 2005
Venue: ABF Conference Centre, Stockholm, Sweden
Organiser: The Swedish Network for Nuclear Disarmament

Managing Nuclear Material Stockpiles in the 21st Century
A conference highlighting the security challenges posed by the large stockpiles of fissile materials and proposing measures for the future.
Time: 3–4 March 2005
Venue: Holmenkollen Park Hotel, Oslo, Norway
Organiser: Norwegian Institute of International Affairs in co-operation with the Norwegian Radiation Protection Authority, with support of the Norwegian Ministry of Foreign Affairs, as a contribution to the WMDC

Elimination of Weapons of Mass Destruction: South Asian Perspectives
A seminar offering Pakistani and Indian perspectives.
Time: 14 March 2005
Venue: India Habitat Centre, New Delhi, India
Organiser: Delhi Policy Group and WMDC

Nuclear Disarmament and Deproliferation
A seminar examining a number of cases of governments which have refrained from acquiring nuclear weapons.
Time: 7 April 2005
Venue: The House of the Estates, Helsinki, Finland
Organiser: The Ministry of Foreign Affairs, Finland and the Weapons of Mass Destruction Commission

Why Do States Abandon Nuclear-Weapon Ambitions?
Workshop in conjunction with the NPT Review Conference
Time: 9 May 2005
Venue: United Nations, New York
Organiser: The Ministry of Foreign Affairs, Finland on behalf of the WMDC

The United Nations Capacity for Monitoring Weapons of Mass Destruction
Workshop in conjunction with the NPT Review Conference
Time: 10 May 2005
Venue: United Nations, New York
Organiser: Permanent Mission of New Zealand to the United Nations on behalf of the WMDC

Iran Nuclear Workshop
Seminar on Iranian Nuclear Capabilities and Motivations
Time: 14 June 2005
Venue: Arundel House, London, United Kingdom
Organiser: International Institute for Strategic Studies and Nixon Center on behalf of the WMDC

Published WMDC studies

The studies are available as pdf-files on the Commission's website: www.wmdcommission.org.

NO. 1 *Review of Recent Literature on WMD Arms Control, Disarmament and Non-Proliferation* by Stockholm International Peace Research Institute, May 2004

NO. 2 *Improvised Nuclear Devices and Nuclear Terrorism* by Charles D. Ferguson and William C. Potter, June 2004

NO. 3 *The Nuclear Landscape in 2004: Past Present and Future* by John Simpson, June 2004

NO. 4 *Reviving the Non-Proliferation Regime* by Jonathan Dean, June 2004

NO. 5 *Article IV of the NPT: Background, Problems, Some Prospects* by Lawrence Scheinman, June 2004

NO. 6 *Nuclear-Weapon-Free Zones: Still a Useful Disarmament and Non-Proliferation Tool?* by Scott Parrish and Jean du Preez, June 2004

NO. 7 *Making the Non-Proliferation Regime Universal* by Sverre Lodgaard, June 2004

NO. 8 *Practical Measures to Reduce the Risks Presented by Non-Strategic Nuclear Weapons* by William C. Potter and Nikolai Sokov, June 2004

NO. 9 *The Future of a Treaty Banning Fissile Material for Weapons Purposes: Is It Still Relevant?* by Jean du Preez, June 2004

NO. 10 *A Global Assessment of Nuclear Proliferation Threats* by Joseph Cirincione, June 2004

NO. 11 *Assessing Proposals on the International Nuclear Fuel Cycle* by Jon B. Wolfsthal, June 2004

NO. 12 *The New Proliferation Game* by William C. Potter, June 2004

NO. 13 *Needed: a Comprehensive Framework for Eliminating WMD* by Michael Krepon, September 2004

NO. 14 *Managing the Biological Weapons Problem: From the Individual to the International* by Jez Littlewood, August 2004

NO. 15 *Coping with the Possibility of Terrorist Use of WMD* by Jonathan Dean, June 2004

NO. 16 *Comparison of States vs. Non-State Actors in the Development of a BTW Capability* by Åke Sellström and Anders Norqvist, October 2004

NO. 17 *Deconflating 'WMD'* by George Perkovich, October 2004

NO. 18 *Global Governance of 'Contentious' Science: The Case of the World Health Organization's Oversight of Small Pox Virus Research* by Jonathan B. Tucker and Stacy M. Okutani, October 2004

NO. 19 *WMD Verification and Compliance: The State of Play* submitted by Foreign Affairs Canada and prepared by Vertic, October 2004

NO. 20 *WMD Verification and Compliance: Challenges and Responses* submitted by Foreign Affairs Canada, October 2004

NO. 21 *Meeting Iran's Nuclear Challenge* by Gary Samore, October 2004

NO. 22 *Bioterrorism and Threat Assessment* by Gary A. Ackerman and Kevin S. Moran, November 2004

NO. 23 *Enhancing BWC Implementation: A Modular Approach* by Trevor Findlay and Angela Woodward, December 2004

NO. 24 *Controlling Missiles* by Jonathan Dean, December 2004

NO. 25 *On Not Confusing the Unfamiliar with the Improbable: Low-Technology Means of Delivering Weapons of Mass Destruction* by Dennis M. Gormley, December 2004

NO. 26 *A Verification and Transparency Concept for Technology Transfers under the BTWC* by Jean Pascal Zanders, February 2005

NO. 27 *Missing Piece and Gordian Knot: Missile Non-Proliferation* by Mark Smith, February 2005

NO. 28 *The Central Importance of Legally Binding Measures for the Strengthening of the Biological and Toxin Weapons Convention (BTWC)* by Graham S. Pearson, February 2005

NO. 29 *Russia in the PSI: The Modalities of Russian Participation in the Proliferation Security Initiative* by Alexandre Kaliadine, August 2005

NO. 30 *Indicators of State and Non-State Offensive Chemical and Biological Programmes* edited by Ingrid Fängmark and Lena Norlander, August 2005

NO. 31 *The 2005 NPT Review Conference: Reasons and Consequences of Failure and Options for Repair* by Harald Müller, August 2005

NO. 32 *National Measures to Implement WMD Treaties and Norms: the Need for International Standards and Technical Assistance* by Andreas Persbo and Angela Woodward, August 2005

NO. 33 *Russia and the Chemical Disarmament Process* by Sergey Oznobistchev and Alexander Saveliev, August 2005

NO. 34 *Transparency and Secrecy in Nuclear Weapons* by Annette Schaper, August 2005

NO. 35 *Multilateral Nuclear Fuel-Cycle Arrangements* by Harald Müller, August 2005

NO. 36 *Nuclear Threat Perceptions and Nonproliferation Responses: A Comparative Analysis* by Scott Parrish and William C. Potter, August 2005

NO. 37 *WMD Crisis: Law Instead of Lawless Self-Help* by Harald Müller, August 2005

NO. 38 *The Relevance of Gender for Eliminating Weapons of Mass Destruction* by Carol Cohn with Felicity Hill and Sara Ruddick, December 2005

NO. 39 *The Influence of the International Trade of Nuclear Materials and Technologies on the Nuclear Nonproliferation Regime* by Dr Vladimir V. Evseev, December 2005

NO. 40 *A Standing United Nations Verification Body: Necessary and Feasible* by Trevor Findlay, December 2005

NO. 41 *Learning from Past Success: The NPT and the Future of Non-proliferation* by Jim Walsh, March 2006

Index